Smart Money Skills for *Parents* of Teens

A Step-by-Step Resource for Parents as they Guide Teens to Financial Freedom

A companion book to "Smart Money Skills for Teens, The Ultimate Guide to Financial Freedom"

Reno Smith

Table of Contents

Introduction

"Do not save what is left after spending; instead, spend what is left after saving."

Warren Buffett

When my daughter was a teen, she came to me with a question that stopped me in my tracks: "How do I save for a car?" It was a simple question, but it opened my eyes to something much bigger. I realized that while our teens are growing up in a world filled with financial decisions, many lack the skills to make those decisions wisely. This sparked my journey to help parents like you guide your teens toward financial literacy.

This book is your companion as you navigate this essential path. It's designed to work alongside my book, **"Smart Money Skills for Teens" ("Teens")**. Together, these resources empower you to teach your children financial skills. The goal is simple: to provide you with the tools to make financial education a part of your family's everyday life.

Statistics paint a clear picture. According to recent studies, only a small percentage of teens feel confident managing money.

Many schools still don't offer personal finance courses. This gap in education makes your role as a parent even more crucial. You have

> *NEW YORK (October 19, 2021) – Financial literacy is low within each of the five generations—the Silent Generation, Baby Boomers, Gen X, Gen Y and Gen Z—but is the lowest among Gen Z, according to a new report by the TIAA Institute and the Global Financial Literacy Excellence Center (GFLEC) at the George Washington University (GW) School of Business.*

the power to shape your teen's financial future, and this book will guide you in doing just that.

Let me introduce myself. I'm a global business executive, an attorney, a former senior government official, a business owner, and, more importantly, a father. Based on my experiences, I believe I have a perspective that can help families achieve financial empowerment. I've experienced the challenges parents face in teaching financial literacy. Through my work, experiences, and research, I've seen firsthand how life-changing financial education can be. And I'm committed to sharing practical advice that you can easily apply in your daily life.

This book is structured to make your journey as seamless as possible. We'll cover topics such as budgeting, saving, investing, and even the role of technology in managing money. Each chapter is designed to build on the last, giving you a comprehensive toolkit to use with your teen and information and insights that might also benefit your financial journey. You'll find exercises, real-life scenarios, and discussion prompts to engage your teen in meaningful conversations about money.

While my first book is a fantastic resource for teens, this book supports you, the parent. Together, these books create a powerful duo that equips you and your teen with the knowledge and skills to succeed. We'll explore ways to integrate the lessons from my **Teens** book into your family's routine, maximizing the impact on your teen's financial literacy.

I encourage you to take an active approach as you work through this book. Have open discussions with your teens. Share your own experiences and learnings. Please encourage them to ask questions and explore their own financial goals. The activities included are designed to be engaging and thought-provoking, fostering a more profound understanding of key concepts.

I also encourage you to take charge of your child's financial education. The benefits extend far beyond understanding dollars, euros, pesos, real, or yuan. You're setting the stage for a future where your teen is confident, informed, less stressed, and empowered to make wise financial decisions. This is a gift that will last a lifetime. So, let's embark on this journey together, ensuring our teens have the skills and knowledge to thrive in a rapidly changing financial landscape.

But before we go... In **Teens***, I provide a bonus chapter on AI, specifically ChatGPT. I did this because I believe utilizing this resource will accelerate learning and executing the information provided.* **Teens** *introduces this with a comprehensive scenario and AI prompts.*

AI is and will continue to be a fundamental factor in our lives, so I believe it is important that we master it as early as possible. But while championing the benefits of AI use, I also caution that overreliance is not recommended and that it can make errors. AI is just one of many tools in our financial toolbox.

Chapter 1

Building a Strong Financial Foundation

The other day, I overheard a conversation between two teenagers at the coffee shop. One discussed how they had just bought the latest smartphone, and the other sighed, admitting they were always broke. It struck me how early financial habits begin and how crucial it is for parents to guide their children in understanding money. This chapter lays the groundwork by helping you understand your financial baseline, a crucial step in building a solid financial foundation for your family and empowering your teens with the necessary knowledge.

Understanding Your Financial Baseline

Daily life requires knowing where you stand financially. It ensures you know your starting point and can plan the best route to your destination. Your family's financial baseline involves assessing **income, expenses, assets, and liabilities**. These elements form the building blocks of financial awareness. So, create your baseline by listing all sources of household income, from salaries to side gigs. Then, track every expenditure, no matter how small, for a few months to get a comprehensive picture of where your money goes. This exercise often reveals surprising patterns, like the cumulative cost of daily coffee runs or streaming subscriptions.

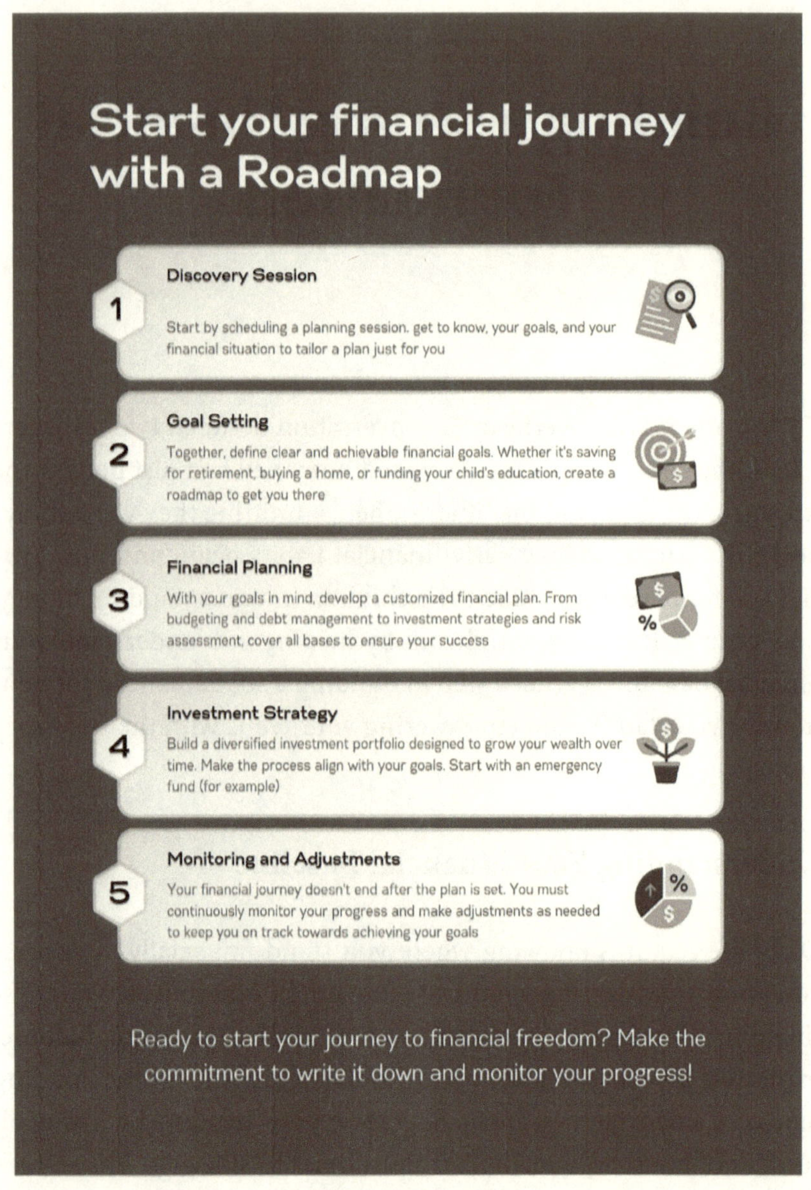

Once you've mapped out your income and expenses, shift focus to your assets and liabilities. **Assets** include anything of value you own, from your home and car to savings accounts and investments. Conversely, **liabilities** are debts and obligations like mortgages, credit card balances, and student loans. Understanding **cash flow**, or the movement of money in and out of your family finances, is essential. Positive cash flow means you're earning more than you're spending, a fundamental goal for financial stability. This awareness lets you make informed decisions about spending, saving, and investing.

Creating a **personal financial statement** is a practical way, at a glance, to see your financial situation. It combines the work above to make your **net worth calculation and an income statement**. Your net worth is the difference between your assets and liabilities. It's a snapshot of your financial health, showing your progress or highlighting areas that need attention. The income statement details your earnings and expenses over a period, helping you understand your financial habits. This statement is not static. Regular updates provide insight into your financial journey, allowing you to track growth and make necessary adjustments. For a detailed guide on crafting this statement, you might find the article "How to Create a Personal Financial Statement" from SmartAsset.

Providing transparency about finances with your family is invaluable. It builds trust, opening the door for honest discussions about money with your teens. Sharing your financial baseline allows them to see the family's financial reality, fostering an environment where they feel comfortable asking questions and learning. This openness isn't to burden them with adult concerns but instead to teach them to appreciate the dynamics of money management. Encouraging these dialogues helps demystify money, transforming it from a taboo topic to a subject of interest and engagement. I did this a little later in life with my children; we all found the experience incredibly valuable.

And I regret that my wife and I didn't do this when our children were in their teens.

Monitoring your financial progress over time is equally important. Consider keeping a **financial journal** to record income, expenses, and net worth changes. This practice keeps you accountable and provides a tangible record of your financial decisions and their outcomes. Additionally, using apps designed for financial tracking can streamline this process. These tools offer real-time insights into your spending habits, helping you spot trends and make informed adjustments. Technology can be a powerful ally in maintaining and understanding your financial baseline, ensuring you and your family remain on a path to financial well-being. We'll reference several later in the book.

Budgeting Basics for Families

Budgeting is the cornerstone of financial management, ensuring our earnings work for us, not vice versa. At its core, a budget is simply a plan for allocating your money, ensuring that every dollar has a purpose. It involves differentiating between **needs** —those essentials like housing, groceries, and utilities — **and wants**, which are the extras that make life more enjoyable. By allocating funds for savings and investments, you secure your family's financial future and teach your teens the importance of financial discipline and foresight.

Creating a family budget may be initially time-consuming, but with a step-by-step approach, it becomes manageable. Begin by setting realistic spending limits for each category in your budget. Take a look at your past expenditures to gauge what limits are feasible. This isn't to cut all enjoyment but to find a balance that allows security and leisure. Involving your teens in these discussions can be particularly beneficial. Not only does it teach them about money management, but it also helps them feel included in family decisions. Discussing why the family might opt for a movie night at home instead of going to the theater can enlighten them.

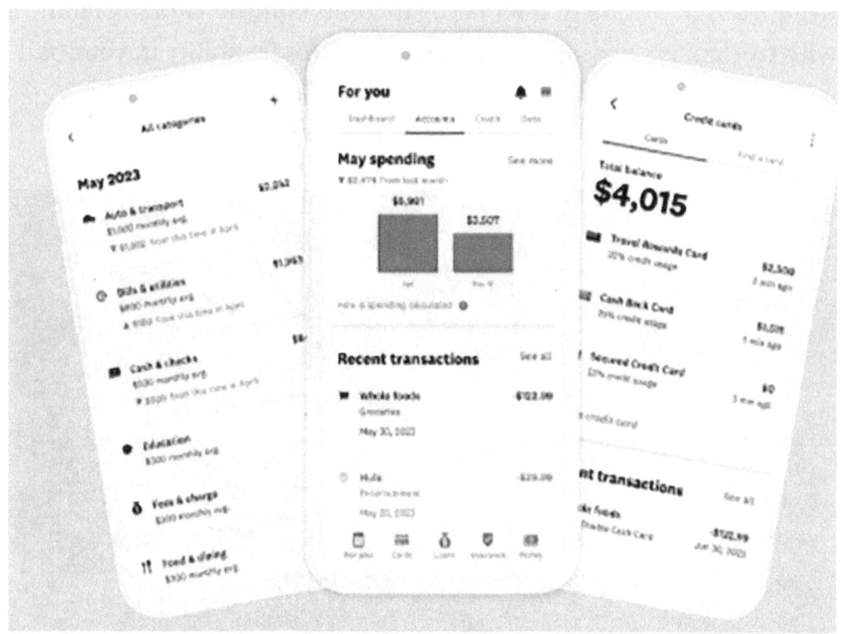

In today's digital age, technology can simplify budgeting significantly. Apps like **Mint** (here) and **You Need a Budget (YNAB)** (referenced in **Teens**) offer robust platforms to track income and expenses, set goals, and even provide educational tools on budgeting. **Mint** provides a comprehensive overview of your bank accounts, credit cards, and bills all in one place, allowing for real-time spending tracking. **YNAB**, on the other hand, offers a proactive approach by encouraging you to plan every dollar before it's spent, fostering a mindset of financial intention. Alternatively, a simple spreadsheet template can be effective, especially for those who prefer a more hands-on approach. These tools provide the transparency and organization needed to maintain a clear financial picture for your family.

Budgeting comes with its own set of challenges. Unexpected expenses, like a car repair or medical bill, can throw even the best-laid plans into disarray. To cope with such surprises, you should include a buffer in your budget or a small emergency fund you regularly contribute to. Additionally, fluctuating income, common among families with freelancers or seasonal workers, requires flexibility in your budget. Adjust your spending categories as needed and prioritize savings during months of surplus to cushion the leaner times.

Action: Budget Worksheet Exercise

Consider setting aside a weekend afternoon to sit down as a family and create a budget together. Use a simple worksheet to list all sources of income and categorize expenses. Discuss what expenses are necessary and which ones are discretionary. As an exercise, challenge each family member to suggest one way to reduce spending or increase savings. This activity fosters teamwork and instills a sense of shared responsibility in managing family finances.

Budgeting is not a one-time task but a continuous process that evolves with your family's needs and circumstances. Regularly reviewing and adjusting your budget teaches adaptability and resilience, crucial lessons for your teens as they prepare to manage their finances. Through this process, they learn that a budget is not a restriction but a roadmap to achieving financial freedom, enabling them to make choices that align with their values and goals.

Setting Financial Goals with Teens

Setting financial goals is pivotal in teaching teens the value of money and the importance of planning. Goals provide direction and purpose, turning abstract concepts into concrete objectives. Understanding the difference between short-term and long-term goals can enlighten teenagers. Short-term goals might include saving for a new tech or a concert ticket, while long-term goals could be toward college tuition or a down payment on their first car. These goals teach patience and delayed gratification and align with personal values, helping teens understand what truly matters to them. When goals resonate with personal interests, motivation naturally follows, making the financial learning process more engaging and rewarding.

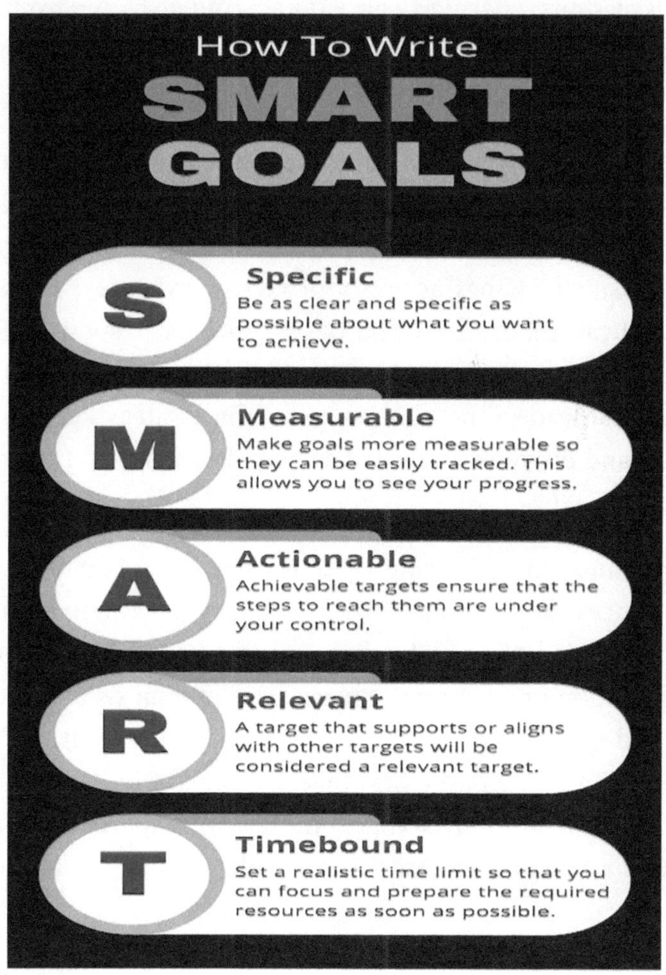

Facilitating goal-setting discussions with your teen can transform an initially challenging task into an empowering experience. Start by introducing the **SMART** goals framework—an effective method for crafting **S**pecific, **M**easurable, **A**chievable, **R**ealistic, and **T**ime-based goals. This framework encourages clarity and focus, making it easier for teens to track their progress and see tangible results. For instance, if a teen wants to save for a laptop, help them break down the cost into manageable monthly savings, ensuring that the goal is realistic given their current income from allowances or part-time work. Regular family financial meetings can serve as a platform for these discussions, offering a space for sharing ideas and exchanging feedback. These meetings can be informal yet structured, providing continuity and accountability.

The possibilities regarding financial goals are vast, but it's important to start with achievable ones relevant to your teen's life. Consider goals like saving for a car, budgeting for a summer vacation, or even starting a small savings account for college expenses. These goals have practical implications and offer lessons in responsibility and foresight. Encourage your teen to set milestones, celebrating small victories that lead to the ultimate goal. This strategy keeps motivation high and provides a sense of accomplishment that fuels further efforts.

A roadmap for achieving these financial goals involves breaking the process into actionable steps. Guide your teen in identifying what needs to be done first, whether opening a savings account or cutting back on unnecessary expenses. Help them set specific milestones and rewards for reaching them. For example, if the goal is to save $500 for a trip, the first milestone might be saving the first $100, with a small reward to boost morale. This approach makes the goal more attainable and teaches valuable lessons in planning and perseverance.

Ultimately, setting financial goals with your teen is more than money. It can build a foundation for future independence and success. By engaging them in meaningful conversations, providing a framework for goal-setting, and supporting them in creating a roadmap, you empower them to take control of their financial future. This process instills confidence and a sense of responsibility, equipping them with skills that will serve them well throughout life. As a parent, I believe our role is guiding, supporting, and celebrating their achievements, fostering a positive and proactive approach to financial literacy.

Creating a Family Spending Plan

A family spending plan is not a budget; it's <u>a blueprint for aligning your financial resources with your family's unique goals and needs</u>. This plan acts as the **guiding framework** to ensure that your family's financial priorities are met while allowing for flexibility and growth. By integrating individual and family goals, you create a holistic approach to managing money that respects the aspirations of each family member. Imagine your teen saving for a personal project while you and your partner focus on building a retirement nest egg. A spending plan *harmonizes* these objectives, ensuring everyone's needs are considered, from the essentials to the little luxuries that make life enjoyable.

When drafting a family spending plan, start by categorizing expenses into essential and discretionary. **Essentials** are the non-negotiable: housing, utilities, groceries, and healthcare. These should take priority, as they form the foundation of your family's security. **Discretionary** spending includes entertainment, dining out, and hobbies. While these are important for maintaining a balanced lifestyle, they should be carefully managed to prevent overspending. By prioritizing essential expenditures, you create a **safety net** that safeguards your family's financial stability, allowing discretionary funds to be used wisely and with intent.

Flexibility is the key to a successful spending plan. Life is unpredictable, as I'm sure you probably know too well, and your financial plan should reflect that. Accommodating changes, whether sudden medical expenses or a spontaneous family getaway, ensures that your plan remains relevant and effective. Planning for emergencies by setting aside a small contingency fund can provide peace of mind when unexpected costs arise. Equally important is allowing room for discretionary spending. This flexibility prevents feelings of restriction and encourages everyone in the family to stick to the plan, knowing there's space for enjoyment and spontaneity within the parameters of your financial strategy.

Involving teens in creating and maintaining the family spending plan can be a powerful educational tool. Assigning them budgeting responsibilities teaches accountability and fosters a sense of ownership over family finances. Encouraging their input on family spending can lead to valuable insights and a deeper understanding of financial priorities. For example, a teen might suggest reducing dining out expenses to save for a family vacation, demonstrating an understanding of trade-offs and the long-term benefits of saving. This involvement nurtures financial literacy and prepares them to manage their own money.

Action: Visual Family Spending Plan

Consider using a simple **template** to draft your family's spending plan. A visual tool can help organize expenses into categories and provide a clear overview of financial priorities. Use color-coding to differentiate between essentials and discretionary spending and include a section for notes where family members can suggest changes or improvements. Displaying this template in a communal area like the kitchen can constantly remind the family of financial goals and commitments.

In crafting a family spending plan, you're not just managing finances but fostering a culture of transparency, collaboration, and strategic thinking. This process equips your family with the tools to navigate financial challenges and opportunities confidently and clearly. As each family member contributes to the plan, they gain a deeper appreciation for the value of money and the impact of their financial choices. For parents, it's a chance to lead by example, demonstrating that financial discipline and flexibility coexist harmoniously. The plan becomes a living document, evolving with your family's changing needs and aspirations and instilling a financial legacy that your teens will carry into their own futures.

Saving for the Future: A Family Approach

Saving as a family is a practice that goes beyond mere financial prudence; it is a collective effort that can foster unity and shared responsibility. When each family member contributes to joint saving goals, it strengthens bonds and instills a sense of achievement that transcends the financial aspect. Consider setting a family goal, such as saving for a vacation or a home renovation. This shared objective teaches financial discipline and highlights the rewards of delayed gratification. In a world that often emphasizes instant pleasure, the art of waiting and working towards a long-term reward is a valuable lesson for teens. They learn that the satisfaction derived from achieving a goal together is far greater than any immediate purchase.

To cultivate effective saving habits, consider implementing strategies that can seamlessly integrate into your family's daily routine.

One practical approach is **automatically** transferring some income from your checking account to a dedicated savings account. This method ensures that a portion of your income is consistently saved, removing the temptation to spend it elsewhere. This is well covered in **Teens**, where apps like **Qapital** are a great resource for "forced" savings. Another method is to create a **family savings challenge**. Set a target amount to save by a certain date and get everyone involved. Perhaps the person who saves the most or comes up with the best cost-cutting idea can choose a family activity. This challenge can make saving fun and competitive, encouraging creative thinking about money management.

Different savings accounts can serve various needs, and understanding these options is crucial for making informed decisions. **High-yield** savings accounts often offer better interest rates than traditional ones, making them a good choice for maximizing savings growth. They provide a safe and accessible place for your money, with the added benefit of earning interest over time. **Certificates of Deposit (CDs)** are another viable option if you have a specific time frame for saving and don't need immediate access to the funds. CDs typically offer higher interest rates in exchange for locking in your money for a set period. Exploring these options can help you choose the best fit for your family's financial goals.

Compound interest is one of the most <u>powerful tools</u> in personal finance, and teaching this to your teens can open their eyes to the long-term benefits of early saving. Compound interest is essentially earning interest on interest, leading to exponential growth over time. The earlier you start saving, the more you benefit from this phenomenon. Consider this simple calculation: if you save $1,000 at an annual interest rate of 5%, you'll have $1,050 after one year. In the second year, you earn interest not just on the initial $1,000 but also on the $50 interest, resulting in $1,102.50. Over time, this compounding effect can significantly increase your savings, illustrating the importance of consistent saving habits. We'll cover this important point in more detail later.

Many families began saving early for their children's college education. By consistently contributing to a high-yield savings account and allowing compound interest to work its magic, they accumulated a substantial fund that covered a significant portion of tuition fees. Such examples demonstrate the tangible benefits of saving and can inspire your family to adopt similar habits. By emphasizing the long-term impact of saving and the power of compound interest, you empower your teens to make informed financial decisions that will benefit them throughout their lives.

The Importance of an Emergency Fund

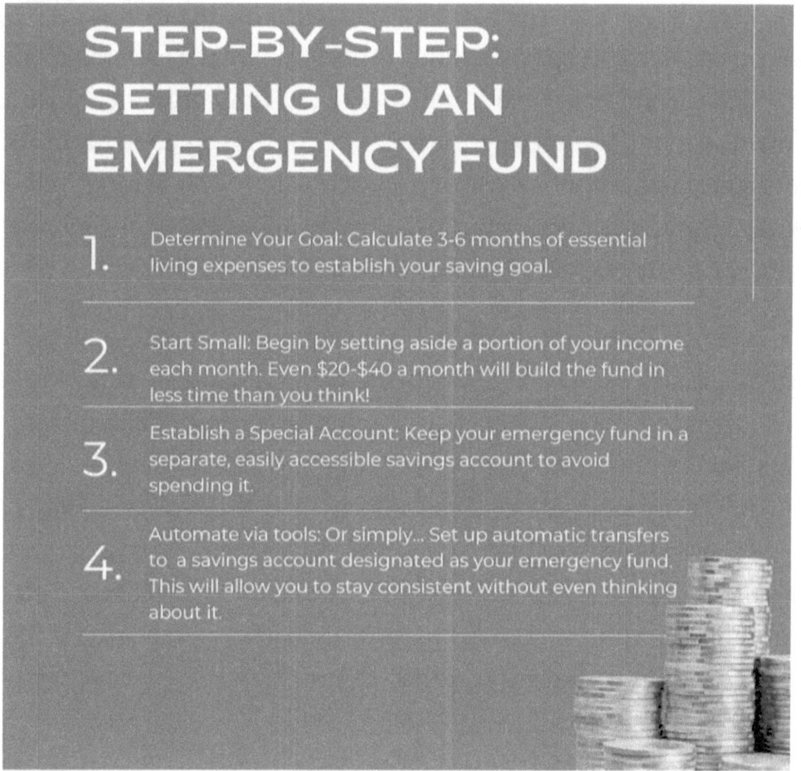

An emergency fund acts as your family's financial safety net, a buffer against life's inevitable surprises. Imagine it's a rainy-day fund for those unexpected moments that can throw your life into disarray, such as sudden medical bills, car repairs, or even a job loss. The purpose of an emergency fund is to provide immediate access to cash without derailing your financial stability or relying on high-interest credit cards. Beyond its practical applications, it offers peace of mind, knowing you're prepared for the unforeseen. This sense of security lets you focus on your family's long-term financial goals without worrying about potential financial pitfalls.

Building an emergency fund starts with setting a clear and achievable target amount. Experts often recommend saving enough to cover three to six months' living expenses, but starting with a smaller goal, like $1,000, can make the process less daunting. Establish a regular savings routine, treating your emergency fund contributions as a <u>fixed expense</u> and non-negotiable in your budget. This practice ensures consistency and helps your fund grow steadily over time. Consider automating transfers to your emergency fund from your checking account so you're not tempted to skip a month. Even small, regular deposits can accumulate significantly, offering protection and financial resilience. **Pay yourself first!**

Despite their importance, misconceptions about emergency funds abound. Some families mistakenly dip into these funds for non-urgent purchases, blurring the line between needs and wants. It's vital to maintain discipline, using the fund solely for genuine emergencies. Another common myth is that credit availability makes an emergency fund unnecessary. However, relying on credit can increase debt, especially if high interest rates apply. On the other hand, an emergency fund keeps you financially independent, mitigating stress and preventing debt accumulation.

The role of an emergency fund in maintaining financial stability cannot be overstated. It is a barrier against the spiraling effect of unexpected expenses, which can quickly lead to borrowing and financial stress. Consider the scenario of a family who faces sudden medical expenses. Without an emergency fund, they will likely have to use credit cards, leading to a cycle of debt that can take years to overcome. In contrast, another family with a well-established emergency fund can manage similar expenses smoothly, preserving their savings and peace of mind. These examples underscore the fund's value and highlight the importance of encouraging teens to contribute. Involvement in building an emergency fund teaches them responsibility and the importance of financial preparedness.

Establishing an emergency fund is crucial in securing your family's financial future. It shields you from life's unpredictability and empowers you to navigate challenges confidently. By prioritizing this financial safeguard, you protect your family and set a positive example for your teens. They learn the value of foresight and planning for the unexpected. This chapter serves as a reminder that building financial security is a collaborative effort that benefits from every family member's active participation and commitment.

Chapter 2

Engaging Teens in Financial Learning

Picture a Saturday morning where the kitchen table is not just a place for breakfast but a battlefield of strategy and wit. This is where my family would often gather for a game of **Monopoly** — a game that, on the surface, is about acquiring properties and money, but at its core, it's a lesson in financial literacy. My teenage son, initially drawn by the allure of becoming a "property tycoon," soon realized the importance of budgeting his play money wisely. This experience becomes more than a game; it transforms into a practical lesson in financial decision-making. It's remarkable how this blend of fun and learning can ignite an interest in financial literacy for the young and old alike.

Incorporating games into financial education can make learning more engaging and enjoyable for teens. Games like **Monopoly** and **Cashflow** offer valuable lessons in money management, investment strategies, and the consequences of financial decisions, all within a playful environment that encourages participation and engagement. These board games simulate real-life financial scenarios, allowing teens to learn by doing, which is often more impactful than passive learning. **Online simulation games** enhance this experience by providing dynamic, interactive platforms where teens can experiment with financial choices in a virtual setting. These games can be tailored to mimic real-world financial situations, offering a safe space for teens to explore the outcomes of their decisions without real-world consequences.

Storytelling offers another effective method of conveying complex financial concepts. By creating fictional characters with relatable financial journeys, you can illustrate abstract ideas in a way that's engaging and easy to understand. Imagine a character who starts with a small savings account and gradually builds wealth through savvy investments and disciplined saving. This narrative can captivate your teen's imagination while imparting valuable lessons about the power of compound interest and strategic financial planning. Sharing personal money stories from successful individuals can also inspire and motivate teens. These stories provide tangible examples of how financial literacy can lead to success, offering inspiration and practical insights.

Creative activities that involve money can further cement these lessons by providing hands-on experiences. Designing a personal budget poster allows teens to visualize their financial goals and the steps needed to achieve them. This project can be as simple or detailed as they like, fostering creativity while reinforcing the importance of budgeting. Crafting a **savings jar** with specific goals provides a tangible reminder of their financial aspirations, encouraging regular contributions and reinforcing the value of saving. These activities make learning tangible and offer teens a sense of ownership over their financial journey.

Organizing **family financial challenges** can also be a powerful motivator for learning. Friendly competitions, such as saving contests with small rewards, can spur interest and engagement. These contests challenge teens to think critically about their spending habits and explore new money-saving ways. Budgeting challenges that simulate realistic scenarios, like planning a family outing on a limited budget, teach valuable lessons about prioritizing and decision-making. Such challenges create a sense of camaraderie and teamwork as family members work together to achieve a common financial goal. This collaborative approach makes financial education a shared experience, fostering open communication and mutual support.

Action: Family Financial Challenge

- Consider setting up a family financial challenge. Each member is given a small budget to plan a weekend activity. The goal is to maximize fun while staying within the budget. Encourage creativity and resourcefulness and discuss the different approaches after the challenge. This activity teaches budgeting skills and promotes teamwork and collaboration within the family.

  Making financial literacy fun and engaging transforms learning from a chore into an adventure. These methods capture your teen's interest and equip them with essential skills for their financial future. As they navigate these activities, they learn to think critically, make informed decisions, and appreciate the value of financial literacy. This chapter encourages you to explore these creative approaches, ensuring financial education becomes a natural and enjoyable part of your family's life.

Action: Money Challenges for Teens

- Imagine your teen planning a **weekend getaway with friends**. They must create a mock budget, considering expenses like transportation, lodging, and meals. This exercise is more than about numbers; it's understanding the real-world implications of financial decisions. By crafting a budget, they learn to prioritize spending, negotiate costs, and adjust plans to fit within their financial limits. This task can spark creativity and strategic thinking as they explore cost-effective alternatives without sacrificing fun. The skills developed here lay the groundwork for managing larger budgets in the future, such as those for college or travel.

- Encouraging teens to **plan a small business venture** provides another avenue for developing financial skills. Imagine them brainstorming a business idea, perhaps a pop-up lemonade stand or a weekend lawn mowing service. They must draft a budget, considering costs for supplies, marketing, and potential profits. This process teaches them to evaluate risks and rewards, fostering an entrepreneurial spirit. It also introduces them to investment and returns, as they learn to allocate resources efficiently. Through this hands-on experience, teens gain valuable insights into the financial aspects of running a business, from managing cash flow to pricing strategies.

- **Collaboration** is key in financial education, and incorporating peer activities can enhance learning through shared experiences. Group projects on financial topics, like researching and presenting different savings accounts, encourage teamwork and communication. Teens learn from each other's perspectives, sharing insights and strategies that broaden their understanding. Peer review sessions for financial plans offer opportunities for constructive feedback as teens critique and refine each other's work. This collaborative approach nurtures a supportive learning environment where teens feel comfortable exploring financial concepts and challenging their assumptions.

- **Role-playing scenarios** provide a safe space for teens to practice financial decision-making. Simulating a job interview for a part-time job, for instance, prepares them for real-life opportunities. They learn to articulate their skills, negotiate salaries, and understand workplace expectations. Another scenario could involve negotiating for a better allowance, where they present a case for increased responsibilities and compensation. These exercises build confidence and communication skills, empowering teens to advocate for themselves financially. By engaging in role-play, they gain practical experience handling financial discussions and negotiations, skills that will serve them well in adulthood.

- **Reflection** is crucial to learning, allowing teens to internalize lessons and improve their financial literacy. Encourage them to journal their experiences, noting challenges faced and solutions discovered. This practice fosters self-awareness and critical thinking as they analyze their financial decisions and outcomes. Group discussions offer another reflection layer, as teens share insights and learn from each other's experiences. These conversations promote a culture of open dialogue, where exploring mistakes and successes becomes a valuable learning tool. Through reflection, teens develop a more in-depth understanding of financial concepts, reinforcing their knowledge and building confidence in their abilities.

Action: Reflection Questions

Consider asking your teen **reflective questions** after completing a money challenge: What was the most difficult part of the task? How did you decide on your priorities? What would you do differently next time? These questions can prompt deeper thinking and understanding, encouraging teens to learn from their experiences.

Using Technology to Enhance Learning

In today's digital age, technology is invaluable for teaching teens about financial management. Using AI is covered a bit in **Teens**. Also, Apps like **Greenlight** and **FamZoo** offer a hands-on approach to learning about money by providing platforms where teens can track their allowances, set savings goals, and even learn about budgeting in a safe, controlled environment. **Greenlight**, for example, comes with a debit card that allows parents to monitor spending and set controls, teaching teens about financial responsibility in real-time. **FamZoo** simulates a real-world banking experience within the family, complete with automatic allowances and customizable financial rules, making it an excellent choice for fostering financial literacy at home. These tools transform abstract concepts into practical skills that teens can apply immediately.

Online courses and resources have become increasingly accessible, offering a wealth of information on personal finance. Platforms like **EdX** and **Coursera** provide courses specifically designed to enhance financial literacy. These classes cover various topics, from basic budgeting to more advanced investment strategies. They are structured to accommodate busy schedules, allowing teens to learn independently. **YouTube** channels dedicated to finance can also be a great resource. They often feature engaging content tailored to younger audiences, breaking down complex financial topics into digestible, entertaining videos. By guiding your teen to these resources, you give them the tools they need to build a strong financial foundation.

For teens who prefer listening to reading, financial podcasts and audiobooks present an ideal solution. Shows like **"Planet Money"** engagingly delve into current economic issues, making complex financial topics accessible and relatable. This format is perfect for teens who might listen while commuting or exercising. Audiobooks focusing on financial basics offer another avenue for learning, allowing teens to absorb information passively while engaging in other activities. The auditory aspect of these resources can capture the attention of teens constantly on the go, integrating financial education seamlessly into their daily routines.

Social media plays a dual role in financial education, serving as a valuable learning tool and a potential distraction. I recommend caution here, but platforms like **Instagram** and **TikTok** can be used to follow financial educators who share tips, advice, and insights in a visually appealing format that is easy to digest. These platforms often feature short, impactful content that can inspire and educate simultaneously. However, it's essential to guide your teen in discerning reliable sources from less credible ones, as the open nature of social media means that not all information is accurate or beneficial. For instance, encouraging participation in finance-related challenges on TikTok can make learning interactive and fun. Still, ensuring that the content is educational and aligns with sound financial principles is crucial.

Technology offers a multitude of opportunities to enhance financial learning for teens. You can create a dynamic and engaging educational experience tailored to your teen's preferences and lifestyle by leveraging apps, online courses, podcasts, and social media. This approach not only makes financial literacy more accessible but also instills a sense of excitement and curiosity about money management. As you introduce these tools to your teen, you're equipping them with the skills they need to navigate the financial aspects of adulthood with confidence and competence.

EXPENSES TRACKER

FIXED EXPENSES	AMOUNT
RENT/MORTGAGE	
ELECTRICITY	
WATER	
GAS	
INTERNET	
PHONE	

FOOD	AMOUNT
GROCERIES	
COFFEE	
SNACKS	

TRANSPORTATION	AMOUNT
FUEL	
MAINTENANCE	
PARKING FEES	
INSURANCE	
PUBLIC TRANSPORT	

ENTERTAINMENT	AMOUNT
MOVIES	
CONCERTS/EVENTS	
HOBBIES	
RESTAURANTS	
PARTIES	
LEISURE TRAVEL	

SHOPPING	AMOUNT
CLOTHES	
ELECTRONICS	
BEAUTY	
HOME GOODS	
GIFTS	

MEDICAL	AMOUNT
DOCTOR VISITS	
MEDICATIONS	
HEALTH INSURANCE	

FITNESS	AMOUNT
GYM MEMBERSHIPS	
SPORTS	
EQUIPMENT	
WELLNESS	
PRODUCTS	

FAMILY & EDUCATION	AMOUNT
CHILDCARE	
TUITION FEES	
BOOKS	
MATERIALS	
COURSES	

SUMMARY	

Real-World Applications: Teens and Money

Daily life has countless opportunities to teach teens about money; many present themselves without much planning. Consider the routine task of **grocery shopping**. It may seem not very interesting, but it's a treasure trove of financial lessons. Engaging your teen in comparing prices between different brands or evaluating the cost-effectiveness of bulk purchases versus smaller quantities instills critical thinking about spending. Discussing the impact of sales and discounts helps them understand the concept of saving. Involving them in creating a shopping list and sticking to a budget can transform an ordinary chore into a practical lesson in money management. These small, everyday decisions build a foundation of financial awareness that teens carry forward into more complex scenarios.

Family meetings offer another platform for financial education. When discussing household bills and expenses, you open a window into real-world living costs. By explaining how utilities, groceries, and entertainment fit into the family budget, you demystify the financial responsibilities that come with adulthood. Involving your teen in these conversations helps them **balance income and expenses**. It's a chance to discuss the importance of setting priorities, planning for future needs, and adjusting spending when unexpected expenses arise. Making these discussions a regular part of family life creates a culture of transparency and shared responsibility, preparing your teen for the financial realities of their future.

Part-time work and internships offer invaluable experiences that extend beyond earning a paycheck. A weekend job in retail, food service, or any other field teaches teens the value of hard work and time management. It instills a sense of discipline and responsibility as they balance work commitments with school and social activities. More importantly, it provides firsthand experience in managing income, budgeting for personal expenses, and setting savings goals. Internships, especially in finance-related fields, offer a glimpse into potential career paths. They provide practical insights into professional environments, networking opportunities, and the chance to apply classroom knowledge to real-world situations. The skills and experiences gained from these roles are instrumental in shaping their financial understanding and career aspirations.

Volunteering for financial literacy organizations can further broaden your teen's perspective on money. For example, **Junior Achievement**, a 100+ year-old global non-profit, provides financial literacy and career experiential learning opportunities to more than 10 million students in 100 countries.

By participating in workshops or community events focused on financial education, teens contribute to a cause while deepening their understanding of financial principles. Teaching others can reinforce their knowledge and highlight the importance of community service. Volunteering at credit unions or similar organizations exposes them to different financial services and operations, offering insights into personal finance management and the broader economic landscape. This experience can foster empathy and a sense of social responsibility as they learn about the financial challenges others face and the impact of financial literacy on community well-being.

Supporting **teen-led financial projects** empowers them to take initiative and apply their knowledge proactively. Organizing a school fundraiser requires planning, budgeting, and marketing—skills directly transferable to real-world financial management. Teens learn to set clear financial goals, manage resources, and evaluate the success of their efforts. Similarly, managing a club's budget introduces them to the intricacies of financial planning and accountability. They develop skills in tracking income and expenses, making informed financial decisions, and communicating effectively with team members. These hands-on projects encourage leadership, teamwork, and problem-solving, equipping teens with the confidence and competence to navigate their financial futures.

Developing a Growth Mindset in Financial Literacy

Imagine your teen staring at their savings account, frustrated by its slow growth. It's easy to become disheartened by setbacks, but adopting a growth mindset can transform these moments into powerful learning opportunities. A **Growth Mindset**, a term popularized by psychologist Carol Dweck, is the belief that abilities and intelligence can be developed through dedication and hard work. In the context of financial literacy, it means embracing challenges as chances to learn, not as roadblocks. When your teen faces financial challenges, please encourage them to see these as opportunities to gain new skills and insights. For instance, if they accidentally overspend their allowance, guide them to analyze what led to this situation and to consider how they might budget differently next time. This approach shifts the focus from failure to improvement, fostering resilience and adaptability.

Encouraging **self-reflection** is a crucial component of developing this mindset. When teens take the time to reflect on their financial decisions, they can better understand their habits and identify areas for growth. Suggest that your teen keep a financial journal to record their spending, savings, and any financial decisions. This practice helps them track their progress and serves as a tool for analyzing past financial missteps without judgment. By regularly reviewing their entries, they can recognize patterns, such as impulse purchases or unexpected expenses, and develop strategies to manage these tendencies. This process of reflection and analysis builds self-awareness and empowers teens to make informed financial choices in the future.

A growth mindset thrives on continuous learning and curiosity. Encourage your teen to seek knowledge beyond the basics of money management. **Introduce them to books** like my **Teens** book that deeply explore financial concepts tailored to their age and interests. Attending workshops and seminars can also spark their curiosity and provide insights into the broader world of finance. These events offer opportunities to engage with experts and peers, further expanding their understanding. By fostering a culture of learning, you help your teen appreciate that financial literacy is not a static skill but a dynamic one that evolves with experience and education.

As a parent, you play a pivotal role in **modeling the behaviors** you wish to instill in your teen. Share your personal growth experiences with money, highlighting how you've learned from mistakes and adapted your financial strategies over time. Perhaps you once struggled with credit card debt but developed a plan to pay it off and now prioritize savings. By openly discussing your journey, you demonstrate that everyone makes mistakes and that growth is possible. Celebrate financial milestones as a family, whether reaching a savings goal or successfully sticking to a budget for several months. These celebrations reinforce the value of persistence and achievement, creating a positive association with financial growth.

Action: Growth Mindset Checklist

Create a simple checklist with your teen to identify areas where they can apply a growth mindset. Include items like "Reflect on a recent financial decision," "Read a new financial book," or "Discuss a financial challenge with a parent." This checklist can serve as a reminder of the steps they can take to foster a growth mindset in their financial journey.

Growth Mindset Financial Checklist for Teens

ACTIVITY	NOTES/PROGRESS
REFLECTION	
Reflect on a recent financial decision you made. - What went well? - What could you improve next time?	
Write down one thing you learned about money management this week.	
Identify one financial mistake you've made and think of a way to avoid it in the future.	
LEARNING	
Read a new financial book or article. - Examples: "Smart Money Skills for Teens" (Reno Smith).	
Watch a video or listen to a podcast about saving, budgeting, or investing.	
Research a financial topic that interests you, like saving for college or starting a side hustle.	
COMMUNICATION	
Discuss a financial challenge or goal with a parent or trusted adult.	
Ask a parent or guardian to explain how they budget or save for big expenses.	
Share one financial success or lesson with a friend.	
ACTION	
Set a weekly financial goal (e.g., save $10, avoid unnecessary spending, etc.).	
Create a simple budget for your allowance or part-time job earnings.	
Track all your spending for one week and identify one area to cut back.	
Start a savings jar or open a savings account.	
GROWTH-ORIENTED PRACTICES	
Write down one financial skill you want to learn and set a plan to achieve it.	
Celebrate a small financial win, like sticking to a budget or meeting a savings goal.	
If something financial doesn't go as planned, write down how you'll adapt or improve next time.	

By instilling a growth mindset in financial literacy, you equip your teen with the tools to navigate the complexities of personal finance confidently. They learn to view challenges as opportunities, embrace continuous learning, and reflect on their experiences, fostering a sense of empowerment and self-awareness. Your guidance and example play a crucial role in shaping their mindset, encouraging them to approach financial literacy as a lifelong endeavor filled with potential for growth and success.

The Role of Parents in Financial Education

Parental involvement in a child's financial education can profoundly impact how they perceive and handle money. You serve as the primary role model in financial behavior, subtly influencing your teen's approach to money management. Demonstrating responsible financial habits provides a live example for your teens to emulate. This goes beyond just budgeting or savings; it illustrates how to make informed financial decisions, manage debt wisely, and understand the value of money. Your actions speak volumes, often more than words can convey, instilling lessons that textbooks alone cannot teach. When you involve them in financial decisions, whether planning a family vacation within budget or choosing between different financial products, you provide them with real-world context. This guidance can help them develop critical thinking and decision-making skills, both essential in financial literacy.

Effective communication about money is key to fostering an open and educational environment. Discussing financial topics openly can demystify the complexities of money management and encourage curiosity. Regular financial discussions can be set at the dinner table, where everyone shares their insights and questions. This practice normalizes financial conversations, breaking down any money-related taboos or discomfort. It's important to create a space where questions are welcomed and explored. Encourage your teens to voice their curiosities, whether about the basics of banking or the intricacies of the stock market. These conversations educate and empower them to take charge of their financial understanding. This ongoing dialogue can also reinforce the learning from other financial literacy activities they engage in, solidifying their knowledge.

Setting **expectations and boundaries** is another crucial aspect of financial education. Clear guidelines help teens learn responsibility and the consequences of their financial choices. Establish rules for money management early on, such as saving a portion of their allowance or earnings, understanding the importance of budgeting, and distinguishing between needs and wants. These rules provide a framework within which they can explore financial independence. Discuss the potential consequences of poor financial decisions, such as overspending or neglecting to save. This conversation should be non-judgmental, focusing on learning and growth rather than punishment. By understanding the impact of their choices, teens develop a sense of accountability and foresight, preparing them for more complex financial decisions. These expectations form the backbone of their financial upbringing, guiding them as they navigate their financial paths.

Sharing personal financial experiences can be one of your most impactful teaching tools. **Transparency about your financial journey**, including successes and challenges, can offer invaluable lessons. Share budgeting techniques that have worked for you, explaining why they were effective and how they helped achieve specific financial goals. Discuss past financial challenges, such as overcoming debt or unexpected expenses, and the solutions you implemented to address them. These stories humanize financial concepts, making them relatable and tangible for your teen. They provide a realistic perspective on financial management, illustrating that everyone faces challenges and that mistakes are part of the learning process. By being open about your experiences, you foster a connection with your teen, encouraging them to learn from your journey and apply those lessons to their own financial endeavors. This dialogue promotes a culture of trust and learning within the family, reinforcing the importance of financial literacy.

As we conclude this chapter, remember that your involvement in your teen's financial education is vital. By modeling responsible financial behavior, opening lines of communication, setting clear expectations, and sharing your experiences, you lay a strong foundation for their financial future. Your role as a guide and mentor is irreplaceable, ensuring they have the tools and confidence to navigate the complexities of finances. And don't forget to make the process fun using the tools provided!

As we move forward, we will explore more strategies and insights to further empower your teen's financial journey, equipping them with the skills needed for lifelong financial success.

Chapter 3

Navigating Credit and Debt

I once sat down with my nephew, who was overjoyed at receiving his first credit card offer. His excitement was palpable as he spoke of the freedom it promised. He imagined dining out, buying the latest tech, and impressing his friends with his newfound purchasing power. Beneath the excitement, there was an obvious misunderstanding of what credit really meant.

At its core, credit is a system that allows you to borrow money with the promise of paying it back later, often with interest. It's the mechanism by which you can access more funds than you currently have, enabling significant purchases or investments. However, <u>this borrowed money isn't free</u>; it comes with the expectation of repayment, typically on a schedule. Understanding this relationship is crucial in teaching teens about financial responsibility. When you borrow, you're essentially entering a contract that obligates you to manage your finances diligently to meet repayment terms.

A solid credit history is vital for unlocking future financial opportunities. It serves as a record of how reliably you pay back borrowed money and is used by lenders to assess your creditworthiness. A good credit history can significantly affect your ability to secure loans, whether for a car, a home, or education. Lenders look for consistent repayment and responsible credit use, which, in turn, influences the interest rates they offer. Higher interest rates can cost you more, making a good credit history essential for financial well-being.

Credit comes in various forms, each with distinct purposes and implications. **Credit cards** provide a revolving line of credit that can be used repeatedly up to a limit, making them suitable for everyday purchases. They can help build credit but require disciplined repayment to avoid accumulating debt. On the other hand, **installment loans** are used for specific purposes like buying a car or financing education, with set repayment schedules over time. <u>Understanding the difference between secured and unsecured credit is also important</u>. **Secured** credit is backed by collateral, such as a home or car, which the lender can claim if you default, while **unsecured** credit relies solely on your creditworthiness.

Teens often have misconceptions about credit that can lead to financial pitfalls. One common misunderstanding is viewing credit limits as spending targets rather than the maximum amount they should borrow. This mindset can lead to overspending and debt accumulation. Another misconception involves minimum payments, where some believe that paying only the minimum due will keep them in good standing. While it might prevent immediate penalties, it also means accruing interest on the remaining balance, leading to higher costs over time. It's crucial to clarify these points to equip teens with a realistic understanding of credit and its responsibilities.

Action: Credit Scenario Exercise

Consider an exercise where your teen maps out a hypothetical month of credit use, including purchases and payments. Ask them to calculate the interest accrued when making only the minimum payments compared to paying the full balance. This exercise highlights the financial impact of different repayment strategies and reinforces the importance of understanding credit terms.

Teaching teens about the proper use of credit promotes financial health and empowers them for a lifetime. By understanding credit's benefits and risks, they can make informed decisions that support their goals. You play a critical role in guiding them through these concepts, ensuring they enter adulthood equipped to manage their finances responsibly. As you navigate these discussions, you're not just teaching them about credit—you're helping them lay the foundation for a secure and prosperous future.

The Credit Score Game Explained

Understanding credit scores is crucial because they are significant in your financial life. Essentially, a credit score is a numerical representation of your creditworthiness, reflecting how likely you are to repay borrowed money. Credit bureaus like **Experian**, **Equifax**, and **TransUnion** in the U.S.A. determine these scores, usually ranging from 300 to 850. They evaluate your credit history and behavior to generate a score lenders use to assess risk. Components of a credit score include payment history, credit utilization, length of credit history, new credit inquiries, and the mix of credit accounts. Each component carries a different weight, with payment history and credit utilization being the most influential. Understanding these elements is vital for maintaining a good credit score, which affects your ability to secure loans and the terms you receive.

Understanding Credit Scores and How to Improve Them

Know the Factors

Credit scores are influenced by payment history, credit utilization, length of credit history, new credit inquiries, and credit mix.

Check Your Credit Report

Regularly review your credit report for errors or inaccuracies that may negatively impact your score.

Pay Bills on Time

Consistently making on-time payments is crucial, as payment history is the largest factor affecting your credit score.

Reduce Credit Card Balances

Aim to keep your credit utilization ratio (the amount of credit you're using compared to your credit limit) below 30%

Avoid Opening Multiple Accounts Quickly

Too many new credit inquiries in a short period can lower your score.

Maintain Old Accounts

Keeping older accounts open can help increase the average age of your credit history, which positively impacts your score.

Diversify Your Credit Mix

Having a mix of credit types, such as credit cards, mortgages, and auto loans, can improve your credit score by showing you can manage various types of credit responsibly.

Understanding credit scores might seem like unraveling a mystery, but it's all based on a straightforward formula! **Payment history** accounts for 35% of your score and records how timely you pay your debts. Consistently late payments can significantly lower your score, while on-time payments build trust with lenders. **Credit utilization**, or the percentage of your credit limits that you're using, makes up about 30% of the score. Keeping this ratio below 30% is advisable to maintain a healthy score. The length of your credit history, contributing 15%, considers the age of your oldest and newest accounts and the average age of all your accounts. **New credit inquiries**, making up 10%, are the number of recent hard credit checks that can temporarily lower your score. Lastly, the **mix of credit**, also 10%, reflects the variety of credit types you manage, such as credit cards, installment loans, and mortgages. This diversity demonstrates your ability to handle different credit forms responsibly.

A strong credit score offers various benefits that enhance your financial standing. With a high score, you're more likely to receive better loan terms, such as lower interest rates, which can save you significant money over time. For instance, a good credit score can mean the difference between affordable monthly payments or financial strain when applying for a mortgage. Additionally, insurance companies often offer lower premiums to individuals with good credit histories, as they are perceived as less risky customers. Beyond loans and insurance, a good credit score can also impact your ability to rent an apartment, as landlords often check credit to gauge financial reliability. Some employers even consider credit scores during hiring, viewing them as an indicator of personal responsibility.

Monitoring and improving your credit score is a proactive step towards financial health. Several free credit monitoring services, like **Credit Karma** or **Credit Sesame**, allow you to track your score regularly, alerting you to changes and potential fraud. These platforms provide insights into the factors affecting your score, helping you make informed decisions. Correcting errors on your credit report is another critical aspect. Credit reports can sometimes contain inaccuracies that negatively impact your score, such as incorrect account balances or payment records. Regularly reviewing your credit report and disputing any errors with the credit bureaus can prevent these issues and protect your score. Additionally, <u>simple habits like paying bills on time, reducing outstanding debt, and avoiding unnecessary credit inquiries can substantially improve your score over time</u>. Understanding and managing your credit score effectively lays the foundation for a stable and prosperous financial future.

Responsible Credit Card Usage

Credit cards, a staple in modern finance, serve as a gateway to financial autonomy for many young adults. They provide a credit line for purchases, subject to repayment with interest. Understanding the terms—interest rates, credit limits, and fees—is essential to use them effectively and avoid unforeseen expenses. Wisely used, credit cards can be instrumental in building a robust credit history, opening doors to future financial opportunities. Yet, without careful management, their convenience can easily foster overspending, underscoring the importance of vigilance in tracking expenditures.

Interest rates on credit cards are a critical factor to consider, as they can significantly increase the cost of borrowing. Credit card interest is typically calculated daily and added to your balance if you don't pay the total amount each month. This can quickly lead to a cycle of debt, especially if you're only making minimum payments. Over time, the concept of compound interest can exacerbate this issue, as interest is charged on both the initial balance and any accumulated interest. Even a small unpaid balance can balloon into a significant debt if left unchecked. Understanding how interest is calculated can motivate responsible card usage, ensuring that payments are made in full whenever possible.

Managing credit cards wisely involves several key strategies that can help prevent debt accumulation. One of the most effective methods is to pay off the full balance each month, avoiding interest charges altogether. This practice saves money and demonstrates responsible credit use, which can positively impact your credit score. Setting spending limits, either mentally or with the help of budgeting tools, can also curb excessive spending. By determining how much you can realistically afford to pay off each month, you can prevent carrying a balance that could lead to financial strain. Additionally, regularly reviewing your credit card statements allows you to track expenses and catch any unauthorized charges early, safeguarding your financial health.

The consequences of misusing credit cards can be severe. Accumulating high debt levels can lead to financial stress and limit your ability to make necessary purchases or investments. High debt levels can also negatively affect your credit score, as they increase your credit utilization ratio—a key component in credit-scoring models. A lower credit score can make securing loans or favorable interest rates more challenging, impacting financial flexibility. Furthermore, the burden of debt can restrict your capacity to save for future goals, such as buying a home or funding education. Understanding these potential pitfalls underscores the importance of using credit cards responsibly, ensuring they remain a tool for building credit rather than a source of financial hardship.

Using credit cards wisely requires discipline and awareness, but they can be a valuable financial tool with careful management. They offer the convenience of deferred payment and can provide rewards or cashback on purchases. However, the benefits of credit cards are only fully realized when used within one's financial means. Teaching teens about these dynamics prepares them for managing credit on their own. By emphasizing the importance of paying balances in full and understanding interest implications, you set the stage for a lifetime of healthy credit practices. Through thoughtful usage, credit cards can enhance financial stability and open doors to future opportunities.

Understanding Loans and Interest

The first time I faced the prospect of taking out a loan, the myriad of options felt overwhelming. Understanding the differences between various types of loans is crucial when guiding teens through the financial landscape. **Personal loans** and **student loans** are two common types that serve distinct purposes. Personal loans are typically unsecured, meaning they don't require collateral and can be used for various expenses, from consolidating debt to financing a home improvement project. They usually come with fixed interest rates, meaning the rate stays the same throughout the loan term, providing predictability in monthly payments. Student loans, however, are specifically designed to cover educational expenses and often offer lower interest rates. They can be federal or private, with federal loans offering benefits like income-driven repayment plans. Understanding these differences helps teens choose the right loan for their needs, balancing flexibility with cost-effectiveness.

Interest rates are pivotal in loan repayments, impacting the total amount paid over time. They are essentially the cost of borrowing money, expressed as a percentage of the loan amount. **Fixed interest rates** remain constant throughout the loan term, providing stability in monthly payments. **Variable interest rates**, conversely, fluctuate with market conditions, which can lead to changes in monthly payments. Understanding how these rates affect loan repayments is essential. Monthly payments are calculated based on the principal amount, interest rate, and loan term. Amortization schedules illustrate how these payments are divided between interest and principal over time, with early payments typically covering more interest. This knowledge equips teens to make informed decisions about loan terms, ensuring affordability over the loan's duration.

Creditworthiness is a key factor in loan approval, influencing the terms and rates lenders offer. A teen's credit profile plays a significant role in determining their loan eligibility. Lenders assess creditworthiness by examining credit scores, payment history, and existing debt. Establishing a credit history can be challenging for teens, often necessitating a co-signer. A co-signer, usually a parent, provides a safety net for lenders by guaranteeing loan repayment. This arrangement can help teens secure loans they might not qualify for independently, but it also places responsibility on the co-signer. A strong credit history can lead to more favorable loan terms, such as lower interest rates and higher borrowing limits, underscoring the importance of building and maintaining good credit habits.

Managing loan repayments effectively is crucial to avoid financial strain. Setting up automatic payments is key, as well as ensuring that payments are made on time and reducing the risk of late fees or negative marks on a credit report. Prioritizing high-interest debt is another important strategy. By first focusing on repaying loans with the highest interest rates, teens can reduce the overall interest paid over time, freeing up funds for other financial goals. Regularly reviewing loan statements and staying informed about the remaining balance and interest rates can help manage repayments effectively. Encouraging these practices instills financial discipline and prepares teens for managing debt in adulthood.

Strategies for Avoiding Debt Traps

Teens today face a landscape filled with potential **debt traps,** and guiding them through these pitfalls is crucial. One of the most insidious traps is **predatory lending practices**. These lenders often target young borrowers with limited credit histories, offering loans with excessively high interest rates and hidden fees. It's essential to educate teens on recognizing these schemes. Warning signs include offers that seem too good to be true or pressure to make quick decisions. Over-reliance on credit cards is another common debt trap. The convenience of plastic money can lead teens to spend beyond their means, especially if they aren't mindful of their purchasing habits. Encouraging them to track their spending can help prevent this issue from spiraling into unmanageable debt.

Teaching teens to live within their means is a **cornerstone** of financial health. This simple principle can shield them from the allure of unnecessary debt. As I have discussed, start by helping them create a realistic budget that accounts for income and necessary expenses, leaving room for savings. Encouraging them to differentiate between needs and wants fosters disciplined spending habits. Building an emergency fund is another vital strategy to avoid borrowing in need. Even small contributions from allowances or part-time jobs can accumulate over time, providing a cushion for unexpected expenses. This practice instills financial discipline and prepares them for life's uncertainties, reducing the temptation to rely on credit in emergencies.

A well-structured **debt repayment plan** can be a lifeline for those already in debt. Two popular methods are the snowball and avalanche approaches. The **snowball method** focuses on paying off the smallest debts first, gaining momentum as each is cleared. This psychological boost can motivate continued progress. Alternatively, the **avalanche method** targets the highest interest debts first, minimizing the total interest paid over time. Both strategies require setting realistic repayment goals, emphasizing consistency and commitment. Teaching teens to prioritize high-interest debt and make regular payments can significantly impact their financial future, freeing up resources for savings and investments.

Financial literacy is the bedrock of avoiding debt. As I have stated, knowledge empowers teens to make informed decisions, preventing common financial pitfalls, especially related to debt management. Engaging in continuous learning fosters a proactive approach to finances, equipping them with the skills to navigate complex financial scenarios. By prioritizing financial literacy, teens build a solid foundation for a secure and prosperous future.

Building and Maintaining Good Credit

Helping your teen establish credit is crucial in setting them up for future financial success. One effective way is by adding them as an authorized user on your credit card account. This method allows them to benefit from your positive credit history without the full responsibility of managing a credit card independently. It's a safe introduction to the world of credit, guiding them in understanding transactions and monthly statements. As an authorized user, they can witness firsthand the importance of paying bills on time and see the impact of responsible credit card use. This experience is a foundational lesson, illustrating how credit works in a controlled environment. It's important to discuss the responsibilities that come with this role, including adhering to spending limits and understanding the consequences of overspending.

Another valuable approach is opening a **secured credit card** in your teen's name. Secured cards require a cash deposit that acts as collateral and sets the credit limit. This setup minimizes risk for the lender and the user, making it a suitable starting point for building credit. Your teen can establish a positive credit history by using the card for small purchases and paying the balance in full each month. These early experiences teach them the mechanics of credit management, like keeping credit utilization low to improve their credit score. As they gain confidence, they learn to manage their finances effectively, laying a solid foundation for future credit use.

Consistent financial habits are key to maintaining good credit. Encourage your teen to make timely bill payments, one of the most significant factors affecting credit scores. Late payments can have lasting negative impacts, so instilling the habit of paying on time is essential. Additionally, keeping credit utilization low—ideally below 30% of available credit — demonstrates financial discipline and boosts credit scores. These practices help your teen develop a strong credit profile, which can open doors to better financial opportunities as they progress into adulthood.

The advantages of maintaining strong credit are numerous and impactful. A high credit score can make it easier to access loans and secure lower interest rates, translating to significant savings over time. It also provides better financial opportunities, like qualifying for premium credit cards with rewards or getting approved for rental properties more easily. These benefits enhance their quality of life and offer financial flexibility.

To support your teen's ongoing credit education, provide them with resources that deepen their understanding of credit management. **Teens** provides this. Fostering a culture of continuous learning will help them build a comprehensive understanding of credit that will serve them well throughout their lives.

Chapter 4

※

Investing Early for Long-Term Success

When my son was twelve, "BayBlade" toys were popular. One day, he approached me with a piggy bank full of coins and asked, "How can I make my money grow?" He didn't have enough saved for the newest version of the toy. I decided to give him the additional funds he needed but saw this as a good opportunity to introduce him to the investing world.

Investing is not just a method to earn money but a strategy for achieving **financial growth and security**. Unlike saving, which involves setting money aside in a safe place, like a bank account, for future use, investing means putting money into assets that have the potential to increase in value over time. This distinction is crucial because saving keeps your money safe, while investing allows it to grow.

However, investing involves **risk** and return. Every investment carries a degree of risk, which is the possibility of losing some or all of the initial investment. At the same time, it offers the potential for **returns** or the gains you make on your investment. Understanding this balance is key to making informed decisions that align with your financial goals.

For beginners, understanding the various types of investment vehicles is essential. Stocks, bonds, and mutual funds are often the starting points for new investors. **Stocks** represent ownership in a company and come with the potential for high returns but also volatility, as their value fluctuates with market conditions. **Bonds**, on the other hand, are fixed-income investments where you lend money to a corporation or government in exchange for interest payments over time. They are generally considered safer than stocks but offer lower returns. **Mutual funds** pool money from multiple investors to purchase a diversified portfolio of stocks, bonds, or other assets, providing an opportunity for diversification and professional management. Another option is investing in real estate, which can offer steady income through rent and potential appreciation over time. **Exchange-traded funds (ETFs)** are like mutual funds but trade on stock exchanges, providing more **liquidity** (easier access to your money) and often lower fees. Each option has its risk and return profile, making choosing investments that align with your risk tolerance and financial goals is important.

Diversification is a fundamental principle in investing, as it reduces the risk of loss by spreading investments across different asset classes. A balanced **portfolio** with a mix of stocks, bonds, and other assets can help manage volatility and protect against market downturns. Not putting all your eggs in one basket minimizes the impact of a poor-performing investment on your overall portfolio. Diversifying within **asset classes** is equally important. For instance, holding stocks from various industries provides a buffer against sector-specific downturns. This strategic approach to investing protects your portfolio and positions it for potential growth, as different assets often perform well under varying market conditions.

Opening an **investment account** tailored for teens is a straightforward process but requires careful consideration. Start by selecting a reputable brokerage platform that offers **custodial accounts**, which an adult manages until the age of majority. This setup allows teens to benefit from investment growth while learning about managing their portfolios. When choosing a brokerage, consider factors like fees, account features, and the availability of educational resources. Once you've selected a platform, decide on the account type. Custodial accounts under the **Uniform Gifts to Minors Act (UGMA) or the Uniform Transfers to Minors Act (UTMA)** allow teens to hold and manage investments under adult supervision. These accounts offer a practical introduction to investing, providing teens hands-on experience while ensuring their investments align with long-term goals.

The Power of Compound Interest

When I first explained compound interest to my daughter, I compared it to planting a tree. You start with a small seed, but over time, with patience and care, it grows into something far greater than its original size. In financial terms, **compound interest** is the interest on the initial **principal** and the accumulated **interest income** from previous periods. This process leads to **exponential growth**, which can significantly increase the value of investments over the long term.

A simple example can help illustrate this: imagine investing $1,000 at a 5% interest rate, compounded annually. After the first year, you'd have $1,050. Instead of withdrawing that extra $50, you leave it in, allowing the next year's interest to be calculated at $1,050 instead of the initial $1,000. Over time, this compounding effect can lead to substantial growth, making it a powerful ally in wealth building.

The difference between **"Simple"** and **"Compound"** interest is significant. Simple interest only earns you money on your initial deposit, while compound interest earns you money on your initial deposit and the interest you've already accumulated. Over time, this can make a huge difference in your savings.

SIMPLE & COMPOUND INTEREST

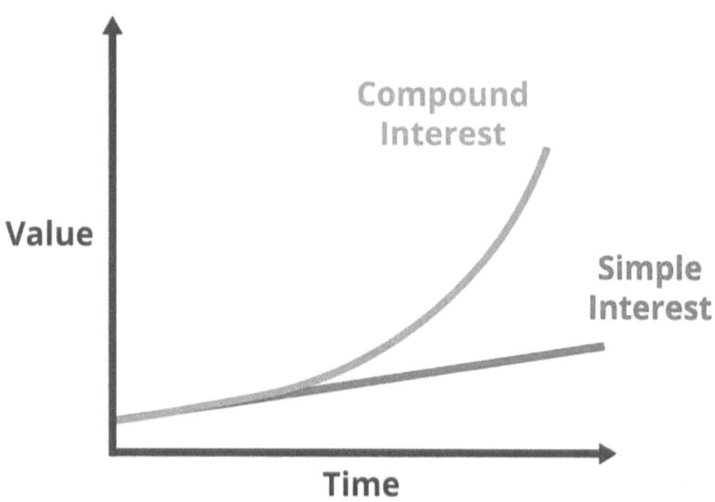

The benefits of compound interest are most pronounced when you **start investing early**. Consider two scenarios: one where an individual begins investing at age 25, contributing $200 monthly to an account with a 5% annual return, and another where someone starts the same investment plan at age 35. By the time the first individual reaches 65, their investment will have grown significantly more than the second, despite contributing the same monthly amount. This difference stems from the additional time the first individual allowed compounding to work its magic. Moreover, reinvesting dividends rather than withdrawing them further enhances compounding's power. Each reinvested dividend becomes part of the principal, accumulating more interest over time and accelerating growth. This simple reinvesting can dramatically amplify the benefits of compound interest, turning modest beginnings into substantial wealth over decades.

Patience and time are the cornerstones of successful investing. The true potential of compound interest unfolds only when investments are left undisturbed for extended periods. Consistently contributing to an investment account, even with small amounts, can yield significant returns over time. Avoiding the temptation to withdraw early is crucial, as it can disrupt the compounding process and diminish potential gains. Just like a tree needs time to mature, investments require a long-term commitment to realize the potential fully. This disciplined approach maximizes returns and instills financial habits that promote stability and growth.

Tracking compound growth is made easier with modern tools and resources. Several online calculators and apps are available to help visualize and monitor investment growth. These tools can provide projections based on interest rates and contribution levels, showing how small changes can impact long-term outcomes. Creating a compound interest projection chart can also be a valuable exercise. By plotting potential growth over time, you better understand how your investments might evolve.

Stocks, Bonds, and Mutual Funds Explained

When discussing investments with teens, stocks often come up first. Owning stock means owning a piece of a company. As a shareholder, you hold rights such as voting on major corporate decisions and receiving dividends, which are portions of the company's profits distributed to shareholders. Stocks can be a lucrative part of an investment portfolio, offering the potential for capital appreciation if the company performs well. However, they are not without risks.

The stock market is inherently volatile, with prices fluctuating based on many factors, from company performance to broader economic changes. This volatility means that while you can make substantial gains, you risk losing your investment. Understanding these dynamics is crucial.

Bonds, on the other hand, function as a more stable investment option. When you purchase a bond, <u>you're essentially lending money to the issuer</u>, a corporation or government, in exchange for periodic interest payments and the return of the bond's face value when it matures. Bonds are generally considered safer than stocks because <u>they offer fixed returns</u> and are less susceptible to market swings. Government bonds, such as U.S. Treasury bonds, are considered particularly low-risk, backed by the government's ability to tax and print money. Corporate bonds typically offer higher yields to compensate for the increased risk than government bonds. This mix of potential returns and stability makes bonds a foundational element of many investment portfolios, particularly for those seeking regular income and lower-risk exposure.

Mutual funds provide a way to <u>diversify investments without managing multiple individual assets</u>. These funds pool money from numerous investors to purchase a diversified portfolio of stocks, bonds, or other securities. <u>Managed by professional fund managers</u>, mutual funds offer an accessible way to gain exposure to a broad range of investments, reducing the risk of investing in a single asset. There are two types of mutual fund management: active and passive. **Active** funds are managed by professionals who make decisions to try to outperform the market. In contrast, **passive** funds, such as index funds, aim to replicate the performance of a specific index, like the S&P 500. Diversification benefits and professional management make mutual funds attractive for novice and seasoned investors.

To make these investment concepts relatable to teens, use analogies that connect with their interests. For example, you can compare owning stock to having a stake in a popular video game company. As game updates can impact a player's experience, company decisions can affect stock value.

Similarly, explain bonds as lending money to a friend with the promise of getting paid back later, with a little extra added, similar to interest.

Also, relating mutual funds to a music playlist can be helpful. Imagine it as a collection of favorite songs (stocks and bonds) curated by a professional DJ (fund manager) to create the best listening (investment) experience.

Connecting these financial concepts to familiar scenarios makes them more tangible and engaging for teens, sparking their curiosity and understanding of the investment world.

Setting Investment Goals with Your Teen

Establishing clear investment goals is like setting the sails before embarking on a journey. It gives direction and purpose to your financial strategies, ensuring every decision aligns with your broader aspirations. Understanding the difference between short-term and long-term goals can enlighten teens. Short-term goals might include saving for a new gadget or a summer camp, while long-term goals could focus on college tuition or building a fund for a gap year. These objectives teach the value of patience and perseverance and help align financial decisions with personal values and interests. Encouraging your teen to think about what they truly want to achieve with their money fosters a sense of ownership and motivation, making the investment process more meaningful and rewarding.

A structured approach to setting these goals can make the process less daunting. The **SMART framework**—**S**pecific, **M**easurable, **A**chievable, **R**elevant, and **T**ime-bound—provides a clear path for crafting realistic and actionable goals. For instance, instead of a vague goal like "Save money for college," encourage your teen to specify an amount, such as "$10,000 over the next four years," and outline the steps needed to achieve it. This might involve setting aside a certain monthly amount from their allowance or part-time job earnings. By breaking down the goal into smaller, manageable steps, your teen can track their progress and celebrate milestones, reinforcing the importance of disciplined saving and investing.

Flexibility is equally important when it comes to investment goals. Life is unpredictable, and financial markets can be volatile, so your teen must learn how to adapt their strategies as circumstances change. Encourage regular reviews of their investment goals, perhaps quarterly or annually, to assess progress and adjust as needed. This might involve reallocating funds based on market conditions or shifting priorities as new opportunities arise. Teaching your teen to be flexible and open to change helps them respond effectively to life's uncertainties and fosters resilience and adaptability, which are essential for successful investing.

Investment goals for teens should be both relatable and inspiring. Consider goals like saving for college tuition, which supports their educational aspirations and teaches them the value of long-term planning. Alternatively, building a fund for a gap year of travel can open their eyes to new cultures and experiences, broadening their horizons and enriching their personal growth. These goals resonate with teens' desires for independence and adventure, motivating them to commit to their financial plans. By aligning investment goals with their interests and passions, you can help them see the tangible benefits of investing, making the process engaging and fulfilling.

Helping your teen set investment goals can guide them to think critically about their future and the steps needed to achieve it. You instill a mindset that values planning, discipline, and adaptability, laying the foundation for lifelong financial literacy. As they navigate the complexities of investing, they'll learn that setting clear objectives is key to making informed, strategic decisions that lead to lasting success.

Navigating Investment Risks

Understanding risk is a fundamental part of investing. Risk, in the context of investments, refers to the possibility of losing some or all of the money you invest. This concept influences every financial decision, as it directly impacts potential returns. There are <u>different types of investment risks</u>, including market risk, credit risk, and liquidity risk. **Market risk** involves the chance that the value of an investment will decrease due to market factors, like economic changes or political events. **Credit risk** is the possibility that a bond issuer will default on their payments. **Liquidity risk** refers to the difficulty of selling an asset quickly without impacting its price. Each type of risk affects investments differently and requires careful consideration when building a portfolio. Recognizing your risk tolerance, or the level of risk you are comfortable taking is crucial. Some people are risk-averse and prefer safer investments, while others are more risk-tolerant and willing to take bigger risks for higher returns. Knowing where you stand helps tailor your investment strategy to suit your financial goals and comfort.

Investors often turn to **asset allocation** and **diversification** to manage and mitigate risks. Asset allocation involves spreading investments across different asset classes, like stocks, bonds, and real estate, to balance risk and reward. By diversifying your portfolio, you reduce the impact of a poor-performing investment, as gains in other areas can offset losses. This strategy is akin to not putting all your eggs in one basket, ensuring that your financial health isn't entirely dependent on a single investment. Another tool for risk management is the **stop-loss order**, which sets a predetermined price at which a security will be sold. This can help prevent significant losses by automatically selling an investment if it falls below a certain value. Through these techniques, you create a safety net that protects against unexpected market downturns while allowing growth.

Research and due diligence are non-negotiable when it comes to investing. Before committing funds, analyzing company financials and market trends is essential. This involves studying balance sheets, income statements, and cash flow statements to assess a company's financial health. Understanding these documents helps you gauge whether a company is stable and likely to grow. For mutual funds, reading prospectuses is vital. These documents outline the fund's objectives, fees, and past performance, providing insight into whether it aligns with your investment goals. Being informed allows you to make decisions based on facts rather than speculation, reducing the likelihood of unpleasant surprises.

Real-world examples illuminate the importance of understanding investment risks. Market crashes, like those in 2008, devastated portfolios heavily weighted in stocks without diversification. Many investors learned the hard way that having a balanced portfolio could have mitigated such losses. On the flip side, consider the success story of an investor who strategically managed risks during turbulent times. Reallocating assets and utilizing stop-loss orders protected their investments from sharp declines, preserving capital that later benefited from market recovery. These cases underscore the necessity of having a risk-conscious strategy, highlighting that while risk is an inherent part of investing, it can be managed effectively with foresight and planning.

Encouraging a Lifelong Investment Mindset

A long-term investment perspective is both a strategy and a mindset that transforms how you approach wealth creation. This perspective emphasizes patience and discipline, two crucial qualities in navigating the financial markets' highs and lows. Focusing on the long haul allows investments to grow and compound over time, maximizing their potential. **Patience** helps you ride out market fluctuations without making impulsive decisions that could derail your financial goals. **Discipline** ensures that you consistently add to your investments, even when it might be tempting to spend or withdraw. This combination of patience and discipline allows the **power of compounding** to work its magic, gradually turning modest contributions into substantial wealth. When you instill this mindset in your teen, you give them the tools to build a secure financial future, safeguarding their ability to achieve long-term goals.

Staying informed and adaptable in changing markets is another critical aspect of a lifelong investment mindset. Financial landscapes are dynamic, and keeping up with financial news and trends is essential. This doesn't mean becoming an expert overnight but rather cultivating a habit of continuous learning. As your teen becomes more knowledgeable and engaged, consider encouraging your teen to read financial articles, watch market updates, and listen to expert analyses. Attending investment seminars and workshops can also provide valuable insights and networking opportunities. These events offer a platform to learn from experienced professionals, discover new strategies, and gain a deeper understanding of market dynamics. These activities empower your teen to make informed decisions that reflect the current economic environment, ensuring their investment strategies remain relevant and effective.

Encouraging an attitude of innovation and opportunity-seeking can transform investing from a routine task into an exciting exploration. Do this by exposing your teen to emerging markets and technology investments. These areas often present new growth opportunities and can appeal to young investors comfortable with change and innovation. Being open to alternative investments, such as sustainable funds or cryptocurrencies, can also broaden their investment horizons. While these options come with their own

<u>risks</u>, they offer the potential for significant returns and align with the innovative spirit of today's youth. By encouraging your teen to think creatively about their investment choices, you foster a proactive wealth-building approach that embraces change and seeks new possibilities.

Mentorship and guidance play an indispensable role in developing a lifelong investment mindset. Learning from seasoned investors provides invaluable insights and shortcuts to understanding complex financial concepts. Encourage your teen to seek mentors who can share their experiences and offer advice and support. These relationships offer perspectives that textbooks can't provide. Joining investment clubs or communities is another excellent way for your teen to connect with like-minded individuals. These groups offer a supportive environment where members can discuss strategies, share successes, and learn from each other's experiences.

Instilling a lifelong investment mindset in your teen sets the stage for sustained financial success. This mindset encourages them to think long-term, remain adaptable, seek out innovation, and learn from others. It's about more than just money— they are building a foundation for a future where they can confidently pursue their goals and dreams. As their financial landscapes evolve, they'll carry these lessons, equipped to make informed decisions leading to prosperity and security. In the next chapter, we'll explore money's emotional and behavioral aspects, further expanding on how to prepare teens for a financially responsible future.

Chapter 5

Emotional and Behavioral Aspects of Money

The other day, I was shopping online, overwhelmed by a sale promising deep discounts on items I didn't need. It was a familiar feeling that I'm sure many of us have experienced—the allure of **retail therapy**. Often considered a harmless indulgence, this term can dig into our financial well-being if left unchecked. For teens, whose emotional landscapes are still forming, the pull of emotional spending can be even more potent. Understanding how emotions drive spending is crucial for helping them develop healthy financial habits. And retailers continue to find ways to make emotions harder to overcome. Currently, the online retailer **TEMU** masters this using gamification as an addictive tool.

Emotional spending is when purchases are driven by emotions rather than necessity. You might recognize it as buying a new outfit after a tough day or indulging in new tech as a reward. Retail therapy, a common form of emotional spending, temporarily lifts mood through the rush of acquiring new items. It can enhance imagination, boost confidence, and even provide a sense of control during times of sadness. However, this behavior often stems from a desire to feel better rather than a genuine need. The pervasive influence of advertising only amplifies this urge, encouraging us to equate happiness with consumption. With their glossy images and compelling narratives, advertisements tap into our aspirations, making it difficult to resist purchasing.

I discuss the consequences of unchecked emotional spending in **Teens,** as it can be severe financially and psychologically. On the financial side, this habit can lead to the accumulation of unnecessary debt. Credit cards make it easy to buy now and pay later. As debts pile up, so does the stress, overshadowing the initial joy of the purchase. Psychologically, emotional spending can result in regret and buyer's remorse. The temporary satisfaction of a purchase quickly fades, leaving a sense of guilt for spending money unwisely. This cycle can become a source of anxiety and a barrier to achieving financial stability.

To help teens recognize and control emotional spending, encourage them to practice mindfulness and self-awareness. Being mindful involves paying attention to the present moment, recognizing emotions as they arise, and understanding their impact on decision-making. <u>Encourage your teen to pause and reflect</u> on their feelings before purchasing. Are they buying because they need the item, or is it an attempt to soothe an emotional need? By identifying these triggers, they can make more informed choices and resist the impulse to spend. Setting financial boundaries and limits is another effective strategy. Encourage teens to establish a personal spending cap for discretionary items, allowing them to enjoy occasional treats without derailing their budget.

Introducing tools to track emotional spending habits can also empower teens to take control of their finances. One effective method is <u>journaling emotions and spending incidents</u>. Suggest they keep a journal to document purchases and the emotions that drove them. This practice fosters self-reflection and highlights patterns that may not be immediately obvious. Reviewing these entries can help them understand the underlying motivations for their spending and develop strategies to manage them. Additionally, apps that categorize spending by emotional triggers can provide valuable insights. These tools often offer alerts and analysis of spending habits, helping teens stay aware of their financial choices and adjust their behaviors accordingly.

Action: Emotional Spending Reflection Exercise

Encourage your teen to complete a reflection exercise by asking them to choose a recent purchase and write about the emotions they felt before, during, and after the transaction. Prompt them to consider whether the purchase was driven by necessity or emotion and how it affected their mood. This exercise can illuminate personal spending patterns and encourage mindful decision-making in the future.

Recognizing and addressing emotional spending is a powerful step toward financial empowerment. By understanding the emotional triggers that influence purchases and implementing strategies to manage them, teens can develop healthier spending habits. This awareness improves their financial health and fosters emotional resilience, equipping them with the skills to navigate the complex landscape of personal finance with confidence and clarity.

Strategies for Financial Discipline

Financial discipline is the cornerstone of a secure and stable future, and cultivating this trait in teens can set them on a path to lifelong financial health. It's about making informed decisions and resisting the allure of impulse purchases. A disciplined approach to money can help avoid the pitfalls of reactive spending, ensuring that financial resources are directed toward meaningful goals. By instilling financial discipline, you're helping your teen build a secure foundation that supports their dreams and aspirations. This discipline mitigates the risk of financial missteps that can lead to debt and stress, clearing the way for a future filled with opportunity and growth.

Teaching teens to create and adhere to a **spending plan** is one practical way to instill disciplined habits. A spending plan acts as a roadmap, guiding them on how to allocate their resources wisely. Encourage your teen to start by listing their income sources, including allowances or part-time job earnings, and then outline their essential expenses. This exercise helps them understand where their money goes and highlights areas where they can cut back. Incorporating **delayed gratification exercises** can further enhance their financial discipline. For instance, suggest they save for a desired item over time instead of buying it immediately. This practice teaches patience and underscores the value of setting and achieving financial goals.

Accountability plays a pivotal role in reinforcing financial discipline. Regular check-ins with a financial mentor or a trusted adult can provide guidance and support, helping teens stay on track with their financial plans. These check-ins offer an opportunity to review progress, discuss challenges, and celebrate successes. Encourage your teen to find an accountability partner for their financial goals. This partnership can be mutually beneficial as they share experiences and strategies for overcoming obstacles. Whether it's a sibling, friend, or mentor, having someone to hold them accountable can make a significant difference in their financial journey, fostering a sense of responsibility and commitment.

Consistency is the bedrock upon which financial discipline is built. Regular practices like consistent saving and budget reviews can solidify financial habits, making them second nature. Encourage your teen to set up a routine for saving a portion of their income, no matter how small. Over time, these savings can grow into a substantial fund, providing a safety net for future needs. Regular budget reviews can reinforce financial discipline by allowing teens to assess their spending patterns and make necessary adjustments. This process of reflection and adjustment helps them stay aligned with their financial goals, ensuring that their actions consistently support their long-term aspirations.

Action: Financial Discipline Checklist

Create a simple checklist for your teen to track their financial discipline practices. Include items like "Update Spending Plan," "Review Savings Progress," and "Schedule Accountability Check-In." This checklist is a tangible reminder of their commitment to financial discipline and helps them focus on their goals.

By embedding these concepts into their daily lives, teens develop a strong sense of financial discipline that will serve them well into adulthood. This discipline not only helps them navigate the complexities of personal finance with confidence but also empowers them to pursue their dreams with the assurance of financial stability. Through consistent effort and support, they can cultivate habits that lead to a secure and prosperous future, free from the constraints of impulsive financial decisions.

Teaching Teens to Manage Financial Stress

The pressures teens face today can be overwhelming, especially regarding financial stress. One of the most common sources of this stress is the pressure to maintain social appearances. Teens often need to keep up with their peers through fashion, tech, or experiences. The desire to fit in can drive them to spend beyond their means, leading to financial anxiety. This pressure is compounded by the influence of social media, where curated images of a seemingly perfect lifestyle can create unrealistic expectations. For teens juggling part-time jobs, managing their earnings adds another layer of complexity. Balancing work commitments with school and social life can be daunting, especially when their income doesn't stretch far enough.

To help your teen navigate these challenges, consider introducing them to **financial mindfulness techniques**. Mindfulness involves being present "in the moment" and aware of one's thoughts and emotions without judgment. Encourage your teen to practice mindfulness when making financial decisions, taking a moment to reflect on their motivations and the potential consequences of their actions. This practice can help them gain clarity and reduce impulsive spending. Additionally, fostering an open line of communication is crucial. Encourage your teen to seek support from you or a trusted mentor when they feel overwhelmed by financial stress. Having someone to talk to can provide reassurance and guidance, helping them find solutions to their problems.

Maintaining a balanced financial life is key to managing stress effectively. Teaching your teen the value of equilibrium between earning, spending, and saving is important. Encourage them to develop time management skills to balance work and study without sacrificing their well-being. I cover this in the Bonus Chapter in **Teens**, where, using AI, they can create a plan to balance work, study, and other activities. Setting realistic financial expectations is also essential. Help your teen understand that it's okay not to have everything their friends have and that building a secure financial future takes time. By setting achievable goals and celebrating small milestones, they can gain confidence and alleviate the pressure to conform to external standards.

Building **emotional resilience** is another important aspect of managing financial stress. Encourage your teen to view financial setbacks as opportunities for growth rather than failures. Every challenge presents a chance to learn and develop new skills. By adopting a growth mindset, they can cultivate resilience and adapt to changing circumstances.

Building a supportive financial network can also be beneficial. Encourage your teen to connect with peers or family members with similar financial goals and values. This network can provide encouragement, share resources, and offer a sense of community. Engaging in regular discussions about money and financial challenges can foster a culture of openness and support, empowering your teen to face financial stress with confidence.

The Psychology of Money: A Teen's Perspective

Teens often view money through a lens shaped by cultural and familial influences, significantly influencing how they perceive and value financial resources. Growing up, children absorb the attitudes and beliefs about money displayed by their parents and community. These early observations can lead them to mirror behaviors, whether a cautious approach to saving or a more relaxed attitude toward spending.

Additionally, as discussed, cultural narratives around success and wealth can color their aspirations, instilling a drive for accumulation or focusing on financial security. Moreover, <u>the impact of social media cannot be underestimated</u>. Platforms like **Instagram** and **TikTok** bombard teens with images of luxury and success, often equating material possessions with happiness and status. This constant exposure can skew their perceptions, making them believe that owning the latest tech or wearing trendy brands is essential for acceptance and self-worth.

<u>Self-identity is intricately linked to financial behavior</u>, influencing teens' choices with money. As they develop their sense of self, many young people begin to associate their worth with what they own. The desire for status and recognition can drive them to purchase items that reflect the image they wish to project to the world. Teens may feel compelled to buy the latest sneakers or tech, not necessarily because they need them, but because they symbolize success and popularity. Understanding this dynamic is crucial for helping them develop healthier relationships with money and avoid defining themselves solely by their purchasing power.

Beneath the surface, subconscious drivers greatly influence financial decisions, often without teens even realizing it. The fear of missing out, commonly known as **FOMO**, is a powerful motivator that can lead to impulsive financial choices. <u>This fear, fueled by social media and peer pressure, pushes teens to spend money on experiences or items simply to avoid feeling left out</u>. Additionally, emotional associations with wealth and poverty can shape financial attitudes. Some teens might view wealth as a means to happiness, while others may see it as a source of stress or conflict, especially if they've witnessed financial struggles in their family. These subconscious beliefs can guide their spending habits and overall financial outlook, impacting their decisions subtly yet profoundly.

Fostering a healthy money mindset in teens involves guiding them to develop a balanced view of finances, prioritizing well-being over material accumulation. Encouraging gratitude and generosity can shift their focus from what they lack to appreciating what they have. By recognizing the value of non-material wealth—such as relationships, experiences, and personal growth—teens learn that happiness isn't solely tied to possessions.

Building self-esteem independent of financial status is equally important. Help teens understand that their worth isn't measured by their bank balance or the brands they wear. Encourage them to pursue interests and activities that align with their values and passions, reinforcing that fulfillment comes from within rather than external validation. This approach cultivates a healthier relationship with money and empowers teens to make financial decisions that reflect their true selves rather than societal expectations.

Overcoming Impulse Buying

Impulse buying is a common behavior, especially among teens, characterized by spontaneous purchases without prior planning. This behavior often emerges from an urge for immediate gratification, driven by excitement or desire rather than necessity. It can accumulate unnecessary items that clutter spaces rather than serve useful purposes. Over time, these impulsive purchases can strain personal budgets, causing financial stress as funds for essential expenses are diverted to satisfy fleeting desires. Recognizing the factors that trigger impulsive buying is crucial in addressing this habit and fostering healthier financial behaviors.

Several psychological and environmental triggers can lead to impulsive purchases. Our **culture of instant gratification**, where everything seems just a click away, plays a significant role. The convenience of online shopping, coupled with algorithms designed to suggest enticing products, makes it easy to fall into the trap of buying on a whim. Emotional states, such as boredom or stress, can also prompt impulsive spending to cope with or escape these feelings. Physical and digital retail environments are meticulously designed to encourage spontaneous purchases through limited-time offers or eye-catching displays, capitalizing on the desire to seize a perceived opportunity before it slips away.

Implementing practical strategies can be highly effective in curbing these impulsive urges. One such approach is establishing a waiting period before making a purchase. Encourage teens to wait at least 24 hours before buying a non-essential item. This pause provides time to reflect on whether the purchase is necessary or just a momentary whim. Additionally, creating a shopping list and sticking to it can help maintain focus during shopping trips, whether online or in stores. By planning purchases in advance and adhering to a list, teens can resist the temptation to stray from their intended spending, reducing the likelihood of impulse buys.

Mindful purchasing is another valuable technique for encouraging conscious spending decisions. Teach teens to evaluate whether a desired item is a need or a want. This distinction helps prioritize spending on essential items over impulsive desires. Encourage them to ask themselves, "Will this purchase satisfy me in the long term, or is it just a temporary thrill?" Assessing long-term satisfaction can prevent regretful purchases that lose their appeal quickly.

By considering the value and utility of potential purchases, teens can make more informed choices that align with their financial goals. This mindful approach fosters a sense of control over spending, empowering teens to make purchasing decisions that reflect their true needs and priorities.

Action: Impulse Buying Reflection

Encourage your teen to keep a small notebook or a digital diary where they record instances of impulse buying. Have them note what triggered the purchase, how they felt before and after, and whether they still value it. Reviewing these entries periodically can help identify patterns and reinforce the practice of mindful spending.

Developing an awareness of impulse buying and implementing strategies to manage it can significantly enhance financial well-being. By understanding the triggers and practicing mindful spending, teens can break free from the cycle of impulsive purchases, paving the way for a healthier financial future. These habits safeguard their budgets and instill a sense of control and intentionality in their financial choices. Through guidance and practice, they learn to appreciate the value of thoughtful spending, ensuring their resources are directed toward meaningful and fulfilling pursuits.

Building Healthy Money Habits

Establishing positive financial habits is one of the most impactful steps to ensure your teen's long-term success. These habits are the building blocks of financial security, each contributing to a stable foundation supporting future growth. Healthy money habits create a sense of financial security by establishing routines that prioritize saving and thoughtful spending. Over time, these habits contribute to the gradual building of wealth. It's not about sudden windfalls or risky ventures but rather a steady, disciplined approach that accumulates resources over time. By instilling these habits early, you help your teen understand the importance of patience and persistence in achieving financial goals. This approach secures their present and paves the way toward a prosperous future.

Starting with the basics, setting up automatic savings contributions can transform savings from a sporadic activity into a consistent practice. Encourage your teen to set up a system where a portion of their income is automatically transferred to a savings account. This approach eliminates the temptation to spend and ensures that saving becomes a routine part of their financial life. Regular financial check-ups and adjustments are also crucial. Just as you might schedule a health check-up, reviewing finances helps identify areas for improvement. Encourage your teen to assess their budget, savings, and expenses periodically. This practice keeps their financial plan aligned with their goals and fosters a proactive attitude toward managing money. These adjustments teach them to adapt to life's changes while staying focused on their objectives. These steps lay the groundwork for a lifetime of financial prudence and adaptability.

Recognizing and rewarding positive financial behavior is an effective way to reinforce good habits. Celebrating financial milestones, no matter how small, can motivate teens to continue their efforts. Whether reaching a savings goal or sticking to a budget for a month, acknowledging these achievements reinforces the value of their hard work.

Consider setting up a rewards system for achieving financial goals. This system can offer incentives for reaching specific targets, such as a special outing or a small gift. You create positive associations with responsible money management by linking rewards to their financial achievements. This practice not only encourages consistency but also adds an element of fun and celebration to their financial journey, making it a rewarding experience.

As we wrap up this chapter, remember that building healthy money habits is as much about nurturing a mindset that values security, growth, and learning in addition to "dollar and sense." These habits equip your teen with the skills needed to thrive financially, ensuring they are prepared for the challenges and opportunities that lie ahead.

In the next chapter, we'll explore how to prepare for future financial independence, providing your teen with the knowledge and tools to transition smoothly into adulthood.

Chapter 6

Preparing for Future Financial Independence

Imagine your teen on the cusp of adulthood, eagerly anticipating their first paycheck from a job they secured through their efforts. This moment represents more than just a financial milestone; it's a pivotal step toward independence. A first job offers invaluable lessons that extend far beyond the paycheck. It builds a work ethic and responsibility, teaching teens the value of commitment and time management. They learn to balance work with other responsibilities, which is essential throughout life.

Moreover, early work experiences expose teens to real-world job expectations, from punctuality to teamwork, providing a foundation for future career success. These initial encounters with the workforce shape their understanding of professional environments, instilling confidence and work ethics that guide them in all future endeavors.

As a parent, guiding your teen searching for job opportunities can be both rewarding and educational. Start by leveraging your own network—family members, friends, and colleagues can be excellent resources for uncovering job leads. Encourage your teen to express their interests and skills, as this can open doors to opportunities that align with their passions.

Additionally, introduce them to job search websites and apps designed for young job seekers. These platforms often feature entry-level positions and part-time work suitable for teens, making the search process more efficient. Teach them to navigate these tools effectively, helping them filter results by location, industry, and required skills. By guiding them in these initial steps, you empower them to take the initiative in their job search, fostering independence and confidence.

Crafting a professional resume and cover letter is an essential skill that will serve your teen well throughout their career. Encourage them to highlight volunteer experiences or extracurricular activities demonstrating valuable skills, such as leadership, teamwork, or problem-solving. These experiences can be as impactful as paid work, showcasing their commitment and ability to contribute positively to a workplace.

Tailoring applications to specific job roles is another crucial aspect of the job search process. Teach them to research potential employers and customize their resume and cover letter to reflect the skills and qualities that each position requires. This attention to detail increases their chances of landing an interview and demonstrates their genuine interest in the role.

Preparing for job interviews can be a nerve-wracking experience for teens, but with the right preparation, they can approach it confidently. Encourage them to practice common interview questions with you or a peer to refine their responses and build confidence.

Questions like "Tell me about yourself" or "Why do you want this job?" are staples in many interviews and practicing them can alleviate anxiety. Emphasize dressing appropriately for interviews, as first impressions are crucial. Even for part-time or entry-level positions, dressing neatly and professionally shows respect and seriousness about the opportunity.

Additionally, remind them to showcase their confidence during interviews. A firm handshake, eye contact, and attentive listening can convey self-assurance and enthusiasm, qualities employers value. By mastering these interview skills, your teen will be well-prepared to make a positive impression and secure their first job.

Action: Resume Building Workshop

Consider organizing a resume-building workshop at home. Provide templates and examples, and work with your teen to create a resume and cover letter. Encourage them to seek feedback from friends or mentors and make revisions based on constructive criticism. This exercise helps them develop a strong application and teaches the importance of seeking and incorporating feedback in personal and professional growth. In the current environment, artificial intelligence tools are proving to be game changers, so consider utilizing that tool as well.

Finding and securing a first job is a transformative experience that sets the stage for financial independence. By guiding your teen through this process, you give them the tools and confidence to navigate the workforce successfully. These early experiences shape their understanding of work and responsibility, laying the foundation for a lifetime of professional growth and achievement.

Managing Income and Expenses

Navigating the world of income management is a crucial skill for teens as they begin to earn their own money. Understanding the difference between gross and net income is the first step. Gross income is the total amount earned before any deductions, while **net income** remains after taxes and other withholdings. Recognizing this distinction helps teens plan effectively, ensuring they know exactly how much money they have to work with. Once they grasp this concept, they can allocate their income wisely, setting aside portions for savings, necessary expenses, and discretionary spending. This practice instills financial discipline and lays the groundwork for future financial stability.

As repeatedly expressed, budgeting is central to managing income effectively. By creating a personal budget plan, teens can ensure their financial stability and avoid the pitfalls of overspending. Start by having them list all sources of income and categorize their expenses, from fixed costs like transportation and phone bills to variable ones such as entertainment and dining out.

Tracking monthly income and expenses helps them understand their spending habits and identify areas where they might be able to cut back. This exercise promotes mindfulness, encouraging them to think critically about each purchase and its impact on their overall financial health. Budgeting helps to make informed choices that align with their financial goals.

Controlling expenses is an ongoing challenge that can be managed with strategic planning. Encourage your teen to identify and cut non-essential expenses, such as impulse buys or subscriptions they no longer use.

Comparing prices and seeking discounts are also practical methods for minimizing unnecessary spending. Whether shopping for clothes, groceries, or electronics, teach them to look for deals and compare prices across different retailers. This habit saves money and instills a sense of value in every purchase. Remind them that being frugal doesn't mean depriving themselves; it means being smart about where their money goes, ensuring it supports their priorities and aspirations.

As we've discussed, technology offers various tools to assist with financial management, making it easier for teens to keep track of their finances. Budget tracking apps like **PocketGuard** can be incredibly useful, providing an overview of their spending and helping them stay within budget. These apps categorize expenditures, offer insights into spending habits, and even suggest areas for improvement. Setting financial alerts for spending limits is another effective strategy, as it provides real-time feedback and helps prevent overspending. By integrating these tools into daily routines, teens can develop good financial habits that foster independence and confidence.

Action: Budgeting Infographic

Create a simple budgeting infographic with your teen that outlines their monthly income, expenses, and savings goals. This visual representation can help them see the bigger picture and adjust as needed. Display it somewhere visible, like on their desk or a family bulletin board, as a constant reminder of their financial commitments.

BUDGET PLANNER

INCOME	AMOUNT

BILLS	AMOUNT

EXPENSES	AMOUNT

DEBT	AMOUNT

SAVINGS	AMOUNT

SUMMARY	AMOUNT
INCOME	
BILLS	
SAVINGS	
EXPENSES	
DEBT	

Managing income and expenses is a vital skill that empowers teens to take control of their financial futures. By understanding their earnings, budgeting effectively, controlling expenses, and utilizing technology, they can navigate their finances with confidence and clarity. These practices prepare them for adulthood's complexities and instill a sense of responsibility and empowerment that will serve them well throughout their lives.

Setting Up a Savings Account

Opening a savings account is a straightforward yet profound step in establishing financial independence for teens. This account is a secure haven that protects funds from the temptations of impulse spending while earning interest over time. The interest accrued may seem modest, but over time, it grows, teaching teens the value of delayed gratification and the benefits of letting their money work for them. This experience introduces them to the concept of compound interest, a powerful ally in building wealth. Additionally, a savings account provides a tangible lesson in financial discipline, encouraging young savers to prioritize long-term goals over immediate desires.

Choosing the right financial institution is crucial for your teen to open a savings account. Banks and credit unions offer varying features, so it's important to compare options. Look for accounts with no monthly fees and low minimum balance requirements, as these are more accessible for young savers. Some institutions even offer special accounts tailored for teens, complete with educational resources and tools to track savings progress. The **Savings Challenge** template is an easy way to begin tracking savings.

Understanding account features and fees is essential. Ensure your teen knows of any potential charges, such as ATM fees or penalties for dropping below a minimum balance. This knowledge empowers them to make informed decisions and avoid unnecessary costs, fostering a sense of responsibility and ownership over their financial choices.

SAVINGS CHALLENGE

SAVING FOR:	GOAL:

MONTH	DATE	DEPOSIT	BALANCE	NOTES
January				
February				
March				
April				
May				
June				
July				
August				
September				
October				
November				
December				

SAVING FOR:	GOAL:

MONTH	DATE	DEPOSIT	BALANCE	NOTES
January				
February				
March				
April				
May				
June				
July				
August				
September				
October				
November				
December				

Maximizing the growth of savings requires strategic planning. We've covered that setting up automatic transfers from a checking account to a savings account effectively ensures regular contributions. This "set it and forget it" approach removes the temptation to skip deposits, making saving a consistent habit. Encourage your teen to treat these transfers as non-negotiable, much like a bill payment. The consistency not only boosts their savings but also ingrains a disciplined approach to money management.

Opting for high-yield savings accounts can further enhance growth. These accounts typically offer better interest rates than standard savings accounts, allowing money to grow more quickly. Although they may require a higher initial deposit, the long-term benefits can be substantial, reinforcing the value of strategic financial planning.

Regular contributions are the lifeblood of a successful savings strategy. Encourage your teen to set specific savings goals for a new gadget, college expenses, or even a car. Clear objectives make saving purposeful and motivate continued efforts, transforming abstract numbers into tangible achievements.

Help them establish a savings schedule that aligns with their income, whether they receive an allowance or earn a paycheck. This schedule should include short-term and long-term goals, providing a roadmap for their financial journey. As they reach milestones, celebrate their achievements, reinforcing the satisfaction of disciplined saving. These experiences lay the foundation for lifelong financial habits, equipping them with the skills and confidence to navigate future financial challenges easily.

Understanding Taxes and Deductions

Taxes are a fundamental part of our financial lives, influencing how we plan and manage our money. Understanding taxes is crucial for teens entering the workforce or earning their first paycheck from a part-time job. Taxes work by taking a portion of income to fund government services like education, infrastructure, and healthcare.

The most common type is income tax, subtracted directly from earnings. Payroll deductions, such as Social Security and Medicare, further reduce take-home pay. These deductions are not arbitrary; they serve specific purposes. Income tax is based on earnings and is subject to various tax brackets. These brackets determine the percentage of income paid in taxes, with higher earners paying a larger percentage. Understanding tax brackets is essential as it helps plan and predict tax liabilities.

Filing taxes doesn't have to be a stressful experience. By breaking the process down into easy, actionable steps, you can conquer your taxes with confidence and ease. For teens, the journey usually starts with gathering necessary documents like W-2 forms, which employers provide to report annual earnings and taxes withheld. These forms are crucial for accurately completing a tax return.

Once the documents are collected, tax software like **Turbo Tax** can simplify filing, guiding users through each step and ensuring compliance with tax laws. These programs often include checks for common errors and explain tax terms, making it easier for first-time filers to navigate the complexities of the tax system. Encouraging teens to use such software streamlines the process and demystifies the often-intimidating world of taxes. It empowers them to take control of their financial responsibilities with confidence.

Deductions and **credits** can significantly reduce taxable income, potentially lowering tax bills. The **standard deduction**, for instance, is a set amount that reduces taxable income, making it unnecessary for many to itemize deductions. This deduction can be particularly beneficial for dependents, often simplifying the filing process. Education-related credits, like the **American Opportunity Tax Credit**, offer further opportunities to reduce taxes by offsetting the costs of tuition, fees, and other educational expenses. These credits are especially relevant for teens pursuing higher education, as they can alleviate some of the financial burdens associated with college expenses. Understanding these deductions and credits is essential for effective tax planning, ensuring teens are not paying more than necessary.

Several resources are available for those eager to deepen their understanding of taxes. The **IRS** website offers a wealth of information specifically tailored for teens, explaining tax fundamentals and offering guidance on various tax-related topics. These resources are designed to be accessible, providing straightforward answers to common questions.

Additionally, tax workshops and seminars can offer hands-on learning experiences. These events often feature experts who provide insights into the tax system, offering tips and strategies for effective tax management. Attending such workshops enhances understanding and provides a platform for asking questions and clarifying doubts. By leveraging these resources, teens can build a solid foundation of tax knowledge, equipping them with the skills needed to manage their finances effectively.

Understanding taxes is a crucial step in achieving financial independence, empowering young individuals to navigate the complexities of adulthood with greater ease and confidence.

Planning for College Expenses

The financial landscape may seem daunting as your teen inches closer to college. Understanding the full scope of college expenses is crucial in preparing you and your teen for what lies ahead. Tuition and fees often represent the most significant portion of college costs, but they are just the beginning. Room and board add significantly, especially if your teen plans to live on campus.

Then there are the costs of books and supplies, which can accumulate rapidly, often catching families off guard. These items, while seemingly minor, can significantly impact the overall budget. Personal expenses, such as transportation and entertainment, must also be considered. Though often overlooked, these daily costs add up over time, painting a complete picture of the financial commitment required for college.

There are several avenues to explore for funding a college education. Scholarships and grants are among the most desirable options as they do not require repayment. Encourage your teen to apply for as many as possible, as each award can lighten the financial burden.

Many scholarships are merit-based, focusing on academic achievement, while others might consider extracurricular involvement or specific talents. Grants, often need-based, provide additional opportunities for financial assistance.

Beyond scholarships and grants, federal and private student loans are standard methods for financing education. Federal loans usually offer lower interest rates and more flexible repayment terms than private loans. Understanding the differences between these loans can help you make informed decisions about borrowing responsibly. While loans can provide immediate relief, it's important to discuss the long-term implications of debt with your teen, ensuring they understand the commitment required to repay these funds after graduation.

Building a college fund is a proactive way to manage future expenses. Consider setting up a **529 college savings plan**, a tax-advantaged account designed explicitly for education teens expenses. Contributions to a 529 plan grow tax-free, and withdrawals used for qualified education expenses are also tax-free, providing a significant financial advantage. Encourage your teen to contribute to this fund, perhaps from part-time work earnings, reinforcing the value of saving and investing in their future. Part-time work provides financial benefits and instills a sense of responsibility and work ethic. By contributing to their college fund, your teen takes an active role in their education, learning valuable financial skills that will serve them well beyond college.

Budgeting for college involves more than just paying tuition; it requires preparation for the entire experience. Estimating living expenses is an essential part of this process. Consider costs such as housing, utilities, groceries, and transportation. These expenses vary depending on whether your teen lives on-campus, off-campus, or at home.

Creating a college budget plan helps anticipate these costs and manage funds effectively. Encourage your teen to participate in this planning process, teaching them to prioritize spending, identify cost-saving measures, and seek student discounts. This exercise not only prepares them for the realities of managing money in college but also empowers them to take control of their financial well-being.

The Journey to Financial Independence

Financial independence represents a pivotal milestone where individuals can sustain themselves without parental support. It involves making informed financial decisions that reflect personal values and future goals. Achieving autonomy goes beyond accumulating wealth; it means living life on your terms, free from financial limitations.

For teens, this journey begins with understanding the significance of financial independence: living without needing financial support from family. This independence fosters a sense of responsibility, empowering them to make wise choices about spending, saving, and investing. It also prepares them for life's uncertainties, equipping them with the skills to navigate financial challenges confidently.

Creating a roadmap to financial independence involves several key steps.

Start by encouraging your teen to explore multiple income streams. This could mean pursuing part-time jobs, freelancing, or even starting a small business. Diversifying income sources boosts earnings and builds resilience against economic fluctuations.

Reemphasize the importance of building and maintaining an emergency fund, a financial cushion that provides security during unexpected events like job loss or medical emergencies. This fund is a safety net, preventing reliance on credit or loans during tough times. By setting aside a portion of their income regularly, teens learn the value of saving for a rainy day, ensuring they're prepared for whatever life throws their way.

Also, reinforce that continuous learning and adaptability are vital components of financial independence. . By embracing a mindset of lifelong learning, they remain adaptable and open to new financial strategies, ensuring they can thrive in an ever-changing world.

Setting long-term financial goals is another crucial aspect of achieving financial independence. Guide your teen in planning for significant milestones such as saving for a home or retirement. Encourage them to visualize their future and identify priorities, whether buying a first house, traveling, or securing a comfortable retirement.

Planning for career advancement is equally important, as it directly impacts earning potential and financial stability. Help them explore paths for professional growth, whether through education, skill development, or networking. Setting clear, achievable goals provides direction and motivation, transforming abstract aspirations into tangible achievements. These goals serve as a roadmap, guiding their financial decisions and ensuring they stay focused on building a secure and fulfilling future.

Financial independence is a journey that requires planning, perseverance, and adaptability. By understanding its significance and taking deliberate steps toward achieving it, teens can gain the confidence and skills to navigate life's financial challenges independently.

They lay the groundwork for a prosperous and fulfilling life by building multiple income streams, maintaining an emergency fund, and setting long-term goals. Continuous learning and mentorship further enhance their capabilities, ensuring they can adapt to changing circumstances and seize opportunities as they arise. With these tools and strategies, teens are well-equipped to embark on the path to financial independence, ready to embrace the freedom and possibilities it offers.

Chapter 7

Real-Life Financial Skills and Applications

Shopping

Think back to the last time you found yourself at the checkout line, glancing over your cart and wondering if you truly needed each item. We've all been caught in the dance between want and need, impulse and intention. Your experience is an opportunity to teach your teen the art of savvy shopping, a skill that can lead to significant savings and financial freedom.

Encourage your teen to adopt the practice of comparing prices across different stores. This habit not only saves money but also teaches critical thinking and patience. With the advent of technology, price comparison has never been easier. Numerous apps allow you to scan barcodes and see how prices stack up at nearby stores. These tools empower your teen to make informed purchasing decisions, ensuring they get the best value for their money.

Additionally, utilizing apps for price matching can further enhance savings. Some retailers offer to match lower prices found elsewhere, reducing the need to shop around physically. By understanding and leveraging these options, your teen can develop a mindset of strategic spending.

One of the most significant challenges in shopping is resisting the lure of impulse purchases. These unplanned buys can quickly derail a budget and lead to buyer's remorse. Teach your teen strategies to resist unnecessary spending, starting with creating a shopping list. This list serves as a roadmap, guiding them through the store and helping them focus on what truly matters.

Encourage them to stick to the list, allowing for flexibility only when necessary. Another effective technique is setting a waiting period for non-essential items. If they find something they want, suggest waiting 24 to 48 hours before purchasing. This pause gives them time to reflect on whether the item is a genuine need or a fleeting desire. Often, the initial urge fades, resulting in a more considered decision.

Introducing your teen to the concept of quality versus quantity is also essential. Understanding the value of purchases is crucial in a world where abundance often overshadows necessity. Teach them to evaluate product reviews and ratings before deciding. These reviews provide insights into the product's performance, durability, and overall satisfaction from those who have already purchased it.

Encourage them to think long-term, considering the item's lifespan and how it fits into their lifestyle. A higher upfront cost may be justified if the product lasts longer and performs better, ultimately saving money over time. This mindset fosters a discerning consumption approach, focusing on items' quality and longevity rather than sheer accumulation.

Coupons and discounts are potent tools in the savvy shopper's arsenal. Show your teen how to find online coupon codes and utilize them to their full potential. Many websites and apps aggregate deals and discounts, making it easier than ever to save on everyday purchases.

Additionally, remind them to take advantage of student discounts at numerous retailers. These discounts often require a simple verification, providing substantial savings with minimal effort.

By incorporating these strategies into their shopping habits, your teen can maximize their purchasing power and cultivate a sense of financial independence.

Family Money

How to Cut Expenses
on Unnecessary Subscriptions

1ST STEP

Make a list of all subscriptions you use, Check your bank and credit card statements to look at what you're paying for

2ND STEP

Call to canceling service, By calling you can talk directly and thoroughly with the customer service.

3RD STEP

Upgrade service
You can go for an upgraded family plan that offers more features, rather than subscribing to more than one service.

4RD STEP

Re-evaluate your usage It especially applies to an annual membership.

Action: Shopping Smart Checklist

Create a "**Shopping Smart Checklist**" with your teen to guide purchasing decisions. Include items like "**Compare three different prices**," "**Check for online coupons**," and "**Evaluate product reviews**." This checklist can be a practical tool they carry with them, reinforcing smart shopping habits each time they purchase.

Understanding Contracts and Agreements

Contracts often seem like a complex web of legal jargon, but they are integral to daily life, especially as your teen steps into adulthood. At their core, contracts are legally binding agreements between parties, outlining the rights and responsibilities involved. Understanding the essential elements of a valid contract is crucial. These elements include offer, acceptance, and consideration. An **offer** is a proposal made by one party to another. **Acceptance** is the agreement to that proposal, and **consideration** is the value exchanged, whether it's money, a service, or something else. Recognizing these components helps demystify contracts, making them more approachable for your teen.

Teaching teens to read and interpret contracts equips them with essential life skills. When faced with a contract, they must identify critical clauses and conditions. These contract parts specify what each party must or must not do. Encourage your teen to read carefully and note any obligations they may agree to. <u>Hidden fees and obligations</u> are common pitfalls that can lead to unexpected costs or responsibilities. Highlight the importance of meticulously checking for such clauses. Understanding complex terms can be challenging but breaking them into simpler concepts can aid comprehension. This practice builds confidence and empowers them to advocate for themselves in contractual situations.

Contracts come in many forms and are encountered in various situations. For teens, mobile phone agreements are one of the first contracts they may encounter. These contracts typically outline the terms of service, including data limits, fees, and penalties for early termination. Part-time job employment contracts are another common type. These agreements specify working hours, wages, and job responsibilities. Understanding these documents ensures that your teen knows what is expected of them and what they can expect in return. Being informed helps them make better decisions and avoid potential pitfalls, whether a phone plan or a job contract.

Before signing any contract, seeking advice from knowledgeable sources is important. Encourage your teen to speak with a trusted adult or mentor who can provide insight into the contract's terms. This person can help clarify any confusing language and ensure your teen fully understands the agreement.

Legal aid services also offer valuable resources for contract review, often providing free or low-cost assistance. These services can benefit more complex contracts, such as those involving significant financial commitments or long-term obligations. Your teen can confidently approach contracts by consulting with experts, knowing they have made informed decisions.

Action: Contract Checklist

Create a "Contract Checklist" for your teen to review agreements. Include items like **"Identify key terms,"** **"Check for hidden fees,"** and **"Consult with a mentor."** This checklist can serve as a practical guide, ensuring they approach each contract diligently and cautiously.

The Basics of Insurance

Insurance may initially appear daunting to you, as well as your teen, but it is essential to protect your finances against unforeseen events. At its core, insurance is about risk management. It involves transferring the potential financial burden of unforeseen events to an insurance company in exchange for a predetermined fee, known as a premium. This fee guarantees that the financial impact on your family is minimized should an adverse event occur, such as a car accident or medical emergency.

Various types of insurance cater to different needs. **Health insurance** covers medical expenses, **auto insurance** protects against vehicle-related incidents, and **renters insurance** covers personal belongings within a rental property. Each type serves a unique purpose but aim to provide financial protection and peace of mind.

Understanding the different types of insurance policies is important for making informed decisions. When selecting a policy, they'll encounter terms like premiums, deductibles, and coverage limits. The **premium** is the amount you pay, often monthly or annually, to maintain the insurance coverage. A **deductible** is the amount you must pay out of pocket before the insurance company contributes to a claim. **Coverage limits** refer to the maximum amount the insurer will pay for a covered loss. These factors vary between providers, making it essential to compare different insurance companies. A teen should learn not only the cost but also the extent of coverage and the company's reputation for customer service. This comparison ensures that the policy aligns with the financial situation and provides adequate protection.

Choosing the right insurance policy requires a thoughtful assessment of personal risk factors. Begin by considering your family's unique needs and potential risks. For instance, additional coverage for those events may be prudent if you live in an area prone to natural disasters. Evaluate policy benefits and exclusions carefully, understanding what is covered and what is not.

Some policies might exclude specific incidents or require additional riders for complete protection. It's essential to read the fine print and ask questions if anything is unclear. This due diligence helps you select a policy that best suits your circumstances, offering comprehensive coverage without unnecessary expenses.

In an incident, knowing how to file an insurance claim is vital. <u>Prompt action can make a significant difference in the outcome</u>. Start by documenting evidence of the incident. Take photographs, gather witness statements, and record relevant details. This documentation supports your claim and helps the insurer understand the situation. Contact your insurance company as soon as possible to initiate the claims process. They will guide you through the necessary steps, including filling out forms and providing additional information. Timely communication and thorough documentation ensure a smoother claims process and increase the likelihood of a favorable resolution.

Action: Insurance Claim Checklist

Consider creating a simple **"Insurance Claim Checklist"** to keep handy in case of an incident. Include steps such as **"Document the incident with photos," "Gather witness information,"** and **"Contact the insurance company promptly."** This checklist is a quick reference during stressful situations, ensuring no critical steps are overlooked.

Renting vs. Buying: A Teen's Guide

As your teen contemplates life beyond the family home, the decision between renting and buying becomes increasingly relevant. Renting and buying each offer distinct advantages and considerations that can significantly impact one's lifestyle and financial future.

Renting is often praised for its flexibility and mobility. It allows individuals the freedom to relocate with relative ease, making it ideal for those who anticipate changes in their career or personal life. Without the long-term commitment of a mortgage, renters can explore different neighborhoods and cities, adapting to new opportunities. However, this flexibility comes with the understanding that rent payments contribute to a landlord's investment, offering no equity or ownership in return.

In contrast, buying a home is often seen as a long-term investment. It allows building equity over time, contributing to personal wealth. Homeownership offers stability and the ability to personalize one's living space. Yet, it requires a significant financial commitment and comes with responsibilities such as maintenance and property taxes. The decision to buy should be carefully considered, considering both the financial implications and the desire for permanence. Discussing these choices with your teen can help them understand the balance between stability and flexibility, aiding them in making a decision that aligns with their future goals.

Assessing readiness for renting or buying involves evaluating personal circumstances, such as financial stability and savings. A steady income sufficient to cover rent and associated living expenses is crucial for renting. Landlords often require proof of income and a credit check to ensure reliability as a tenant. When considering buying, the financial requirements are more substantial. A stable job, a good credit score, and significant savings for a down payment are essential. Assessing housing needs is equally important. Renting may be more practical if your teen foresees a short-term stay in an area. Conversely, buying could offer greater financial benefits if they plan to settle long-term.

The process of renting a property starts with searching for rental listings, which can be found online or through local real estate agents. Potential rentals should be visited to assess their condition and surroundings. Once a suitable property is found, understanding the lease agreement is critical.

A lease outlines tenancy terms, including the duration, rent amount, and property rules. Encourage your teen to read the lease thoroughly, paying attention to terms regarding deposits, maintenance responsibilities, and penalties for early termination. Understanding these details protects their interests and ensures a positive rental experience.

If buying is the chosen path, saving for a down payment is a significant first step. Typically, this requires 20% of the home's purchase price, although options exist for lower down payments with additional mortgage insurance.

Understanding **mortgage** basics is crucial. A mortgage is a loan used to purchase a home, requiring monthly payments over several years. These payments include principal and interest, and the interest rate can vary based on the loan's terms. **Fixed-rate mortgages** offer consistent payments, while **adjustable-rate mortgages** may fluctuate. Your teen needs to understand these options and choose a mortgage that aligns with their financial situation and long-term plans. Encourage them to consider the total cost of homeownership, including taxes, insurance, and maintenance, as they evaluate their readiness to buy.

Renting and buying have unique implications for lifestyle and finances. Helping your teen navigate these differences equips them with the knowledge to make informed choices. Whether they choose the flexibility of renting or the investment of buying, understanding the responsibilities and opportunities of each path ensures they are prepared for the next steps in their journey toward independence.

Navigating Financial Aid and Scholarships

As your teenager prepares for higher education, understanding financial aid is crucial. Education costs can be high, but several funding options are available.

Grants and scholarships are desirable because they don't require repayment and are often awarded based on need or merit. In contrast, student loans must be repaid with interest, so they should be approached carefully due to long-term financial implications.

Work-study programs also provide an option, allowing students to earn money through part-time campus jobs, helping cover living expenses while gaining work experience.

Guiding your teen through the scholarship research and application process is important. Start by using scholarship databases to find various opportunities based on criteria like academic achievement and extracurricular activities. Encourage them to apply for both national and local scholarships.

Writing strong scholarship essays is essential. These essays should highlight your teen's unique experiences and goals, tailored to each specific scholarship prompt. A well-written essay can help your teen stand out, boosting their chances of obtaining funding.

The application process for financial aid involves several steps, beginning with completing the **Free Application for Federal Student Aid** (**FAFSA**). This application determines eligibility for federal aid, including grants, loans, and work-study programs. It's essential to fill out the FAFSA accurately and submit it as early as possible to maximize aid opportunities. Once submitted, your teen will receive a financial aid award letter from each college they apply to, detailing the types and amounts of aid offered. Understanding these letters can be challenging, so take the time to review them together, comparing offers and considering factors like the total cost of attendance and any unmet needs. This comparison will help your teen decide which schools are financially viable options.

Meeting application deadlines is vital in the financial aid process, as missing them can lead to lost funding opportunities. Help your teen create a timeline for scholarship applications, FAFSA submissions, and any additional forms required by colleges. Set reminders to ensure nothing is missed. Encourage them to start early, allowing time to gather documents and write essays. Staying ahead of deadlines reduces stress and shows responsibility, which appeal to scholarship committees.

Navigating financial aid and scholarships can initially seem overwhelming, but with careful planning and persistence, your teen can secure the funding needed for their education. This process teaches valuable organization, perseverance, and financial literacy lessons, setting the stage for future success.

Building a Personal Budget: A Teen Project

Imagine your teen standing at the threshold of financial independence. The key to this door is a personal budget, a powerful tool that helps manage money effectively. A budget is a plan that ensures funds are allocated to cover various expenses, from necessities like food and transportation to discretionary spending on hobbies or outings. It also includes allocating money for savings, building an emergency fund, and providing a safety net for unexpected expenses.

To help your teen create a budget, start by identifying all sources of income, such as allowances, part-time job earnings, and gifts. Next, assist them in tracking monthly expenses, categorizing them into fixed costs (like phone bills) and variable costs (such as dining out). This will clarify where their money goes and reveal potential savings.

Encourage them to set realistic savings goals, whether for a new gadget or a college fund. By defining these goals, they can tailor their budget to consistently save, fostering good financial habits.

As discussed, in today's digital age, numerous tools and resources can streamline budgeting. Apps like **Mint** and **PocketGuard** offer intuitive interfaces for tracking income and expenses, making budgeting accessible and enjoyable. These apps help categorize spending, alert users to upcoming bills, and visualize their financial health with graphs and charts. For those who prefer a more hands-on approach, creating a budget spreadsheet can be just as effective. Encourage your teen to experiment with both methods to see which one works best for them. These tools simplify budgeting and offer valuable insights into spending patterns, enabling your teen to make informed financial decisions.

Regularly reviewing and adjusting a budget is crucial, as financial situations can change rapidly. Encourage your teen to set aside time each month to analyze their spending habits. They should identify areas of overspending and opportunities to cut back, allowing them to modify their budget accordingly. This practice fosters a proactive approach to money management, helping your teen adapt to changes and maintain financial control. Developing this habit will build essential skills as they approach adulthood.

As you guide your teen through building and managing a personal budget, you're Teaching teens to budget equips them with essential life skills, fostering discipline and the ability to set and achieve goals. This process not only helps them manage money but also instills responsibility and independence. By learning to prioritize needs and make informed decisions, teens lay a foundation for future financial success. In this chapter, we explored key financial skills for adulthood. Next, we'll discuss creating a financial legacy to benefit future generations.

Chapter 8

Creating a Financial Legacy

I remember sitting at the kitchen table with my parents, poring over the family budget. It wasn't just about numbers; it was about values. My father would talk about the importance of saving, while my mother emphasized giving back. Though seemingly mundane, these conversations instilled a deep understanding of our family's financial values. They taught me that every dollar we spent or saved reflected our beliefs. As parents, you can pass down these lessons to your teens, shaping their financial habits and character. By embedding financial values into your family's ethos, you cultivate a legacy that transcends material wealth, fostering responsibility and ethical behavior in the next generation.

Family financial values serve as the guiding principles that shape decisions and behavior. They provide a framework for understanding the importance of responsibility and accountability. When you instill these values in your children, you equip them with the tools to make informed choices. It's about teaching them that financial decisions are not just about personal gain but also about contributing positively to society. Ethical financial practices, such as honesty and fairness in transactions, have become second nature. This ethical grounding helps teens navigate financial challenges with integrity and foresight, ensuring they make choices that align with their values. By emphasizing these principles, you lay the groundwork for a financial legacy prioritizing ethical considerations over mere profitability.

Open discussions about money beliefs and values within the family are essential to reinforce these values. You can foster communication by dedicating time to weekly family financial meetings. These gatherings provide a platform for discussing financial goals, challenges, and successes. Encourage storytelling sessions where family members share lessons learned from financial experiences, both good and bad. These narratives educate and strengthen family bonds, creating a shared understanding of the values that drive financial decisions. Making these discussions a regular part of family life creates an environment where financial literacy flourishes, and every member feels empowered to contribute their insights and ideas.

Aligning family values with financial goals requires deliberate effort and thoughtful planning. Start by creating a family mission statement articulating your core beliefs and aspirations. This statement acts as a compass, guiding financial decisions and ensuring they reflect your family's values. Involve every family member in this process, allowing them to express what matters most. This inclusion fosters a sense of ownership and commitment to the mission. Once established, set value-driven financial goals that align with the mission statement. These goals might include saving for a family trip to a culturally significant location or investing in community projects. You create a cohesive strategy that aligns with your family's vision by tying financial activities to values.

To solidify these values, engage in activities that reinforce them. Organize family workshops on money management where you can explore different financial strategies and their implications. These workshops provide an opportunity to delve deeper into specific topics, such as budgeting or investing, and to assess how they align with your family's values. Another effective exercise is developing a family financial values charter. This document outlines the principles that underpin your family's financial philosophy, serving as a tangible reminder of your commitments. Encourage each family member to contribute, ensuring the charter represents the diverse perspectives within your household. Engaging in these activities creates a living testament to your family's values, guiding financial decisions and fostering a sense of unity and purpose.

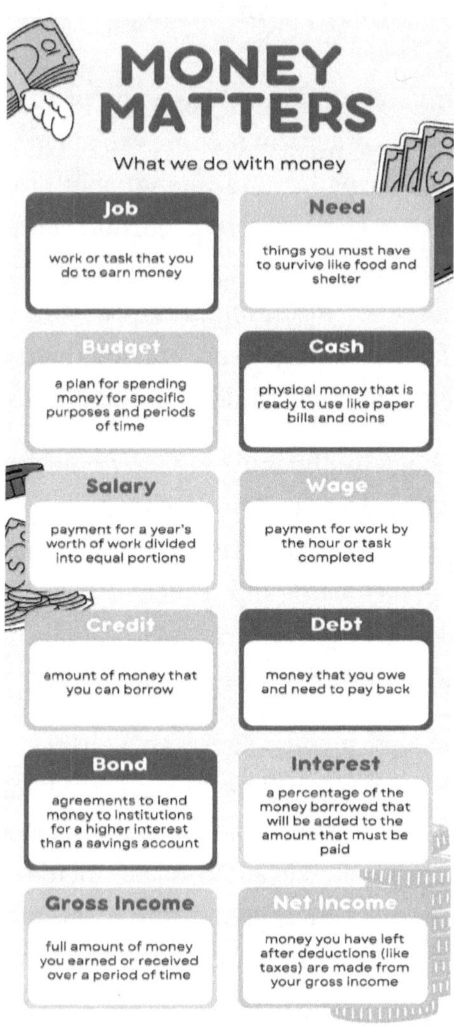

Action: Family Financial Values Charter

Consider creating a Family Financial Values Charter together. Gather around the table and brainstorm the most important values to your family. Write them down and discuss how they influence your financial decisions. This charter can be displayed in a common area as a reminder of your shared commitments.

Teaching Philanthropy and Giving

One afternoon, my son came home from school excited about a charity drive his class was organizing. As he explained it, I realized how philanthropy could shape his understanding of money and responsibility. Teaching teens about giving nurtures empathy and social awareness. Engaging in philanthropic activities helps them grasp the interconnectedness of their community and the impact they can have. This awareness fosters empathy, encouraging them to consider how their actions affect others and build vital community connections.

Teens can engage in philanthropy in various ways, such as volunteering at local food banks, tutoring, or participating in clean-up projects. These activities provide immediate benefits and help develop skills like teamwork and leadership. Additionally, encouraging them to donate a portion of their earnings teaches financial planning and the importance of charitable giving.

Creating personal giving plans can enhance their efforts. By setting aside a percentage of their income for donations, teens can make philanthropy a consistent part of their financial lives. Supporting causes they are passionate about makes them feel more invested and motivated, transforming giving into a meaningful experience and reinforcing their commitment to making a difference.

Philanthropy's impact on personal growth profoundly shapes teens' character in lasting ways. Through volunteering, they develop leadership skills, learn to take initiative, make decisions, and inspire others. These experiences often increase confidence and self-esteem as teens see firsthand the difference they can make. Moreover, engaging in philanthropic activities broadens their perspective on social issues, exposing them to diverse communities and challenges. This exposure fosters critical thinking and problem-solving skills as teens learn to navigate complex social dynamics and contribute creatively to solutions. Philanthropy encourages them to look beyond their immediate environment and consider how they can contribute to the greater good, cultivating a sense of purpose and direction in their lives.

Action: Personal Giving Plan Exercise

Encourage your teen to develop a personal giving plan. Have them research different charities and causes that interest them. Ask them to choose a few to support and decide on a percentage of their income to donate regularly. This plan can be reviewed and adjusted as their interests and financial situation evolve.

Preparing Teens for Unexpected Financial Challenges

Life is full of surprises, and financial challenges are no exception. These issues can arise unexpectedly, whether due to an economic downturn or a sudden personal setback. It is essential to prepare your teen for such eventualities. A good starting point is helping them understand the reality of economic fluctuations. Market dynamics can change rapidly due to political shifts, natural disasters, or technological advancements. These changes can affect everything from job security to the cost of goods and services.

Teens need to grasp how these external factors can impact their personal finances. Recognizing personal vulnerabilities is also crucial. Encourage your teen to assess their financial situation and identify areas where they may be exposed to risk, such as depending too much on a single source of income. This awareness lays the foundation for building financial resilience, enabling them to make informed decisions and take proactive steps to protect their financial well-being.

To build financial resilience, it is essential to implement strategies that help withstand setbacks. One practical approach is to diversify income streams. Encourage your teen to explore part-time jobs, freelance work, or even small entrepreneurial ventures. This diversification not only increases their income but also provides a safety net in case one source of income diminishes.

Another key strategy is to maintain flexible financial plans. Teach your teen to adapt their budget and financial goals in response to changing circumstances. Flexibility allows them to adjust their spending, saving, and investing habits without compromising their long-term financial stability. By fostering these habits, you empower your teen to face economic challenges with confidence and preparedness.

Problem-solving skills are essential for overcoming financial challenges. Encourage your teen to develop critical thinking abilities that will benefit them during tough times. Conducting financial scenario planning is a valuable exercise. Have them envision potential challenges, such as losing a part-time job or facing unexpected medical expenses, and brainstorm possible solutions. This exercise not only enhances their problem-solving skills but also builds confidence in their ability to handle real-world financial issues.

Additionally, practicing decision-making under pressure is crucial. Encourage them to simulate high-stakes situations where they must make quick financial decisions with limited information. These scenarios help them learn to weigh options, assess risks, and make informed choices, even when under stress.

Practical exercises can greatly help prepare for unexpected financial challenges. One effective activity is role-playing emergency scenarios, where your teen navigates sudden expenses or income drops, exploring different strategies and outcomes.

Another useful exercise is developing a mock crisis response plan. Guide your teen to outline steps for financial emergencies, including accessing emergency funds, reassessing budgets, and seeking additional income.

These activities equip your teen with valuable skills and insights, fostering resilience and resourcefulness in handling financial challenges.

Action: Emergency Scenario Simulation

Consider organizing a hypothetical emergency scenario simulation with your teenager. Present a situation where they suddenly lose a significant portion of their income and must adjust their budget accordingly. Encourage them to identify areas where they can cut back, explore alternative sources of income, and develop a step-by-step response plan. This exercise will enhance their problem-solving skills and boost their confidence in managing financial challenges independently.

Encouraging Entrepreneurial Thinking

Imagine a world where your teen sees possibilities everywhere, where they view challenges as opportunities to innovate. This mindset lies at the heart of entrepreneurship, a powerful force that fosters creativity and independence. Being an entrepreneur means more than starting a business; it's about embracing change and taking risks to create something new. It encourages young minds to think outside the box, to question the status quo, and to dream big. This spirit of innovation drives personal growth and contributes to societal advancement. Through entrepreneurship, teens learn to rely on themselves, building an invaluable sense of autonomy in any career path. They also gain the ability to adapt and thrive, crucial skills in today's ever-changing world.

Leadership and team-building abilities are at the forefront, as entrepreneurs must guide and inspire others to bring their vision to life. Working collaboratively with a team, they learn to communicate effectively, resolve conflicts, and harness diverse talents to achieve common goals. Financial literacy and budgeting expertise are equally important. Entrepreneurs must understand how to manage resources wisely, make informed financial decisions, and plan for future growth. By mastering these skills, teens enhance their entrepreneurial potential and gain a deeper understanding of personal finance. This knowledge empowers them to make sound financial choices, whether managing a startup or their personal budget.

Starting small ventures provides a practical way for teens to explore entrepreneurial opportunities and apply their skills. Begin by helping them identify market needs and niches. Encourage them to observe their surroundings and ask questions like, "What problem can I solve?" or "What service can I improve?" This approach sharpens their analytical skills and opens their minds to new possibilities.

Once they have a clear idea, guide them in developing a simple business plan. This plan should outline their goals, target market, and strategies for success. Encourage them to consider potential challenges and devise solutions to overcome them. By going through this process, teens gain valuable experience in planning, decision-making, and strategic thinking, which lays the groundwork for future entrepreneurial success.

Encouraging participation in programs and resources designed for aspiring entrepreneurs can greatly support their entrepreneurial journey. Youth entrepreneurship workshops provide hands-on experiences, allowing teenagers to learn from industry experts and connect with like-minded peers. These workshops typically cover essential topics such as business development, marketing, and financial management, offering a comprehensive understanding of the entrepreneurial landscape.

Additionally, participating in school business clubs is an excellent way for teens to enhance their skills. These clubs offer a platform for students to collaborate on projects, pitch ideas, and compete in local or national competitions. Through these activities, teenagers build confidence, expand their knowledge, and gain practical experience that prepares them for future entrepreneurial endeavors.

Planning for Generational Wealth

Generational wealth is more than just passing down money; it's about ensuring that future generations have the financial security and opportunities to thrive. It involves building a legacy to provide for your descendants and preserve your family's values and achievements. At its core, generational wealth creates a safety net for your children and grandchildren, allowing them to pursue their dreams without worrying about financial instability. It means laying the groundwork today so your family can enjoy the fruits of your efforts for years to come. This legacy, built on the principles of hard work and strategic planning, not only supports financial security but also serves as a testament to your family's enduring values and commitments.

Diversifying your investments across various asset classes is crucial to build and sustain generational wealth. This approach spreads risk and increases the growth potential, as different assets react differently to market conditions. Consider investing in stocks, bonds, real estate, and alternative assets like commodities or art. Each offers unique benefits and challenges, and a well-balanced portfolio can capitalize on strengths while mitigating risks.

Establishing family trusts and estates is another effective strategy. These legal structures protect your assets and ensure they are distributed according to your wishes. Trusts can offer tax advantages, preserve wealth through generations, and provide a structured way to support family members who may not be financially savvy. By carefully planning and managing your investments, you create a robust foundation that can withstand economic fluctuations and provide lasting benefits for your descendants.

Education plays a crucial role in sustaining generational wealth. It's not enough to simply accumulate assets; you must also equip your heirs with the knowledge and skills to manage and grow that wealth. Encouraging continuous learning and adaptation will help future generations navigate an ever-changing financial landscape.

As stated, consider enrolling your children in financial education programs that provide a solid understanding of personal finance, investment strategies, and economic principles.

Intergenerational financial discussions are equally important. By opening lines of communication, you foster a culture of transparency and collaboration, allowing family members to share insights, strategies, and lessons learned. These discussions enhance financial literacy and reinforce the values and goals that underpin your family's wealth.

Successful families often show how generational wealth can endure through careful planning and strategic decision-making. For instance, multigenerational businesses that have thrived for decades succeed by adapting to market changes, embracing innovation, and maintaining strong governance structures. They understand the importance of nurturing talent within the family, ensuring that each generation is prepared to lead and manage the business.

Additionally, lessons from family financial advisors provide valuable insights. Advisors typically emphasize the need to set clear goals, maintain disciplined investment strategies, and prioritize long-term growth over short-term gains. They promote a balanced approach that considers the immediate needs of family members while preserving wealth for future generations. By learning from these examples and applying these principles, you can create a lasting legacy that benefits your family for years to come.

Generational wealth encompasses more than just the financial assets you pass down; it also includes the values, knowledge, and opportunities you offer to your descendants. Achieving generational wealth requires careful planning, strategic investments, and a commitment to education and communication. By emphasizing these elements, you can create a legacy that empowers future generations to thrive, preserves your family's heritage, and ensures continued success.

Celebrating Financial Milestones Together

Reaching a financial milestone is worth celebrating. Celebrating these achievements is vital, not just for the thrill of reaching the top but for the motivation that comes with recognizing how far you've come. Celebrating financial successes reinforces positive financial behaviors, encouraging everyone in the family to keep striving. It builds confidence, especially for teens, as they see tangible results from their efforts. This boost in self-esteem can be a powerful motivator, driving them to set even higher goals and work diligently toward them. Recognizing these achievements is like giving your family a pat on the back, saying, "Well done, let's keep going."

Celebrations don't have to be grand to be meaningful. Consider hosting a family milestone party. It could be a simple gathering at home where each member shares their personal financial achievement. Maybe it's saving for a new bike or completing a budgeting course. This celebration can include a special dinner or a family game night, focusing on spending quality time together.

Another idea is to create a financial achievement scrapbook. Here, you can document each milestone with photos, notes, and reflections. Over time, this scrapbook becomes a cherished family heirloom, a visual reminder of all you've accomplished together. It's a tangible way to appreciate the journey—every challenge faced and every goal met.

After the celebration, it's crucial to channel that momentum into setting new goals. Reflect on past successes and the lessons learned along the way. What strategies worked? What could be improved? This reflection focuses on using mistakes as part of growth.

Encourage everyone to think about their next financial aspirations. Whether saving for a college fund, planning a family vacation, or starting a new investment, having a fresh goal keeps the motivation alive. Setting new targets and creating plans to achieve them fosters a mindset of continuous growth and progress, which is essential for long-term financial well-being.

Family support plays an instrumental role in reaching financial milestones. Sharing success stories within the family strengthens bonds and inspires. When one member achieves a goal, it encourages others to pursue their dreams. This collective encouragement creates an environment of positivity and mutual support.

Offering mentorship and guidance for new goals is equally important. As parents, your experience and insights can be invaluable to your teens. Guide them through setting realistic objectives, developing action plans, and staying committed. Your support and belief in their abilities can be the difference between hesitation and action, helping them confidently navigate their financial paths.

Celebrating financial milestones is not just about the achievements; it's about the journey, lessons learned, and personal growth. It's about fostering a culture of encouragement, where each success builds the foundation for future endeavors.

Remember the importance of pausing to celebrate as your family continues to set and reach new goals. In these moments of reflection and recognition, you solidify the values and habits that will sustain your family's financial legacy for generations to come. And as you turn the page to the next chapter of your financial story, carry forward the spirit of celebration and the promise of what's yet to be achieved.

Conclusion

"It's not about how much money you make, but how much money you keep, how it works for you, and how many generations you keep it."

Robert Kiyosaki

As we reach the end of this journey, I recognize that we've covered a lot of important ground. So, let's take a moment to reflect on the core purpose of this book. It is a companion to my book, "Smart Money Skills for Teens," designed <u>to empower you</u>, the parent, in teaching financial literacy to your teens. By providing the tools and guidance needed, this book aims to make financial education an accessible and engaging experience for the entire family.

Throughout the chapters, we've explored a variety of key topics. We began by laying the groundwork for a solid financial foundation, emphasizing the importance of understanding and managing finances from an early age. We delved into the essentials of budgeting, helping you create a family-friendly plan that includes everyone, especially your teens. We also discussed the significance of setting financial goals, teaching your teens the value of saving and planning for the future. And we purposely revisited important elements.

The book's vision is to be a practical tool for fostering financial literacy and empowerment within your family. We've aimed to create an informative and engaging learning experience using real-world examples and interactive elements. The dialogue guides are designed to facilitate open and meaningful conversations with your teens about money, helping to demystify financial concepts and build trust.

Some of the key takeaways from this book include the importance of teaching your teens how to budget effectively, the basics of investing for long-term growth, and the responsible use of credit. These are crucial skills that will serve them well throughout their lives. By imparting this knowledge, you help your teens develop confidence in managing their finances and making informed decisions.

Now is the time to take action. I encourage you to apply the strategies discussed throughout the book actively. The benefits of financial literacy are long-term and far-reaching, providing your teens with the foundation they need to achieve financial independence and success. By starting these conversations now, you are setting them up for a future where they can confidently navigate the financial world.

Continuous learning and adaptation are key. As the financial landscape evolves, so too should our understanding and approach. Encourage your teens to be curious and proactive in their financial education journey. Learn alongside them, embracing a mindset of lifelong learning that will benefit them and you as a family unit.

Inspiring a positive financial legacy is perhaps the most rewarding aspect of this endeavor. By instilling financial wisdom and values in your teens, you are ensuring they are equipped to face the challenges and opportunities of the financial world with confidence. Your guidance and support are invaluable, and the impact of your efforts will resonate through generations.

Finally, I want to express my heartfelt gratitude for your commitment to enhancing your family's financial literacy. Your role in shaping your teens' financial futures is significant, and your dedication is commendable. Thank you for embarking on this journey with me and for empowering your family with the knowledge and skills needed for a prosperous financial future.

Representative References

- *How to Create a Personal Financial Statement* https://smartasset.com/financial-advisor/personal-financial-statement

- *How to Set S.M.A.R.T. Financial Goals (With Examples)* https://finmasters.com/smart-financial-goals/

- *Best Budget Apps for Families (2024): 7 Tools to Manage ...* https://marriagekidsandmoney.com/best-budget-apps-for-families/

- *Emergency Fund: What it Is and Why it Matters - NerdWallet* https://www.nerdwallet.com/article/banking/emergency-fund-why-it-matters#:~:text=Why%20do%20I%20need%20an,help%20you%20avoid%20borrowing%20more.

- *Gamification for financial education: building resilience ...* https://www.undp.org/es/argentina/blog/gamification-financial-education

- *The Best Money Apps for Kids and Teens* https://www.allcards.com/best-money-apps-for-kids-and-teens/

- *Spreading Financial Literacy Through Storytelling* https://www.linkedin.com/pulse/spreading-financial-literacy-through-storytelling-jay-rehak

- *Parents' Role in Economics and Personal Finance Education* https://www.stlouisfed.org/education/parents-role-education

- *Teaching Teens About Credit* https://www.dollargeek.com/credit-score/teaching-teens-about-credit/

- *7 Ways Your Credit Score Affects Your Financial Health* https://www.firstexchangebank.com/7-ways-your-credit-score-affects-your-financial-health/

- *How to Use a Credit Card Responsibly: 10 Tips* https://www.capitalone.com/learn-grow/money-management/tips-using-credit-responsibly/

- *How I Helped My Young Adult Build Credit Smartly And ...* https://www.forbes.com/advisor/credit-cards/how-i-helped-my-young-adult-build-credit-smartly-and-avoid-debt-traps/

- *BOOK REVIEW: Smart Money Strategy* https://www.thesenior.com.au/story/8102549/book-is-right-on-the-money/

- *Investing for Teens: What They Should Know* https://www.investopedia.com/investing-for-teens-7111843

- *The Power of Compound Interest: Calculations and ...* https://www.investopedia.com/terms/c/compoundinterest.asp

- *Understanding The Different Types Of Investment Vehicles* https://www.bankoncube.com/post/understanding-the-different-types-of-investment-vehicles

- *Can Retail Therapy Actually Be Helpful?* https://www.verywellhealth.com/retail-therapy-5217208

- *How can a teen manage/overcome financial anxiety and ...* https://www.quora.com/How-can-a-teen-manage-overcome-financial-anxiety-and-stress

- *The Impact of Social Media on Teen Spending Habits* https://investorscabin.com/articles/the-impact-of-social-media-on-teen-spending-habits

- *How to stop your teen from impulsive spending* https://www.gohenry.com/uk/blog/financial-education/how-to-stop-your-teen-from-impulsive-spending

- *Teen employment hit a 14-year high in 2023 - Marketplace.org* https://www.marketplace.org/2024/01/29/teen-workforce-rise/#:~:text=According%20to%20the%20Labor%20Department%2C%20about%20250%2C000%20more%20teens%2C%20ages,highest%20annual%20rate%20since%202009.

- *The Best Money Apps for Kids and Teens* https://www.allcards.com/best-money-apps-for-kids-and-teens/

- *How to open a bank account for a minor* https://www.usbank.com/bank-accounts/how-to-open-a-bank-account-for-a-minor.html

- *Understanding Taxes - Teacher Site* https://apps.irs.gov/app/understandingTaxes/teacher/

- *A Review of Financial Literacy for Millennials* https://alair.ala.org/bitstreams/8ef44147-b76e-430f-8b66-aecb5b88e6ee/download

- *Money-Saving Apps for Teens: Budgeting, Tracking, and ...* https://www.azcentralcu.org/blog/money-saving-apps-for-teens/

- *How to Make Agreements with Teens: A Step by Step Guide* https://courtneyharriscoaching.com/making-agreements-with-your-teenagers-and-children/

- *12 Top Financial Aid Tips and Tricks for College Students* https://www.umassglobal.edu/news-and-events/blog/top-financial-aid-tips-and-tricks

- *Family Education: Why Aligning on Values is Critical to ...* https://www.sequoia-financial.com/family-education-why-aligning-on-values-is-critical-to-sustaining-generational-wealth/

- *Teaching Teens About Philanthropy and Charitable Giving* https://ascent.usbank.com/private-capital-management/ascent-resources-and-insights/next-generation-wealth/teaching-kids-about-philanthropy.html

- *Building Financial Resilience: Strategies for Overcoming ...* https://www.acclaimfcu.org/building-financial-resilience-strategies-for-overcoming-financial-stress/

- *9 Entrepreneurship Programs for Teens* https://www.bostontechmom.com/9-entrepreneurship-programs-for-high-school-students/